THE BEST BREAD BOOK

This book is the result of a life-long interest in breadmaking. Patricia Jacobs has collected and adapted recipes from all over the world, and has created many delicious original recipes herself. She holds cookery classes in her Sussex home.

She has travelled widely and while living in Africa regularly contributed cookery articles to newspapers. Among her other interests is music, in which she has a degree from the London Royal Academy.

Patricia Jacobs is married to Professor Jake Jacobs of Sussex University, and has two children. All the recipes in this book have been tried and approved by her family.

THE

Patricia Jacobs

BEST BREAD BOOK

Everything you need to know about traditional breadmaking,
together with many delicious new recipes created by the author

Pan Books London and Sydney

Other cookery books available in Pan

Kathleen Broughton **Pressure Cooking Day by Day**

Savitri Chowdhary **Indian Cooking**

Gail Duff **Fresh all the Year**

Gay Firth and Jane Donald **What's for Lunch Mum?**

Theodora Fitzgibbon **A Taste of Ireland A Taste of London A Taste of Scotland A Taste of Wales A Taste of the West Country Crockery Cookery**

Michel Guérard **Cuisine Minceur**

Robin Howe **Soups**

Rosemary Hume and Muriel Downes **The Cordon Bleu Book of Jams, Preserves and Pickles**

Enrica and Vernon Jarratt **The Complete Book of Pasta**

George Lassalle **The Adventurous Fish Cook**

Kenneth Lo **Quick and Easy Chinese Cooking Cheap Chow**

Claire Loewenfeld and Philippa Back **Herbs for Health and Cookery**

edited by R. J. Minney **The George Bernard Shaw Vegetarian Cook Book**

edited by Bee Nilson **The WI Diamond Jubilee Cookbook**

Marguerite Patten **Learning to Cook**

Jennie Reekie **Traditional French Cooking**

Constance Spry and Rosemary Hume **The Constance Spry Cookery Book**

Katie Stewart **The Times Cookery Book The Times Calendar Cookbook**

Marika Hanbury-Tenison **Deep-Freeze Sense**

First published in Great Britain 1975
by Harwood-Smart Publishing Co Ltd
This edition published 1978 by Pan Books Ltd,
Cavaye Place, London SW10 9PG
2nd printing 1978
© Patricia Jacobs 1978
ISBN 0 330 25519 3
Illustrated by Marcus Rutherford
Bread board motifs on pages 5, 27, 47, 69, 89, 91 and on
'Recipe Created by Author' by GM Graphics
Design and typesetting by GM Graphics (Northwood)
Printed and bound in Great Britain by
Richard Clay (The Chaucer Press) Ltd, Bungay, Suffolk

To my family
who courageously ate their way
through all these recipes

CONTENTS

INTRODUCTION

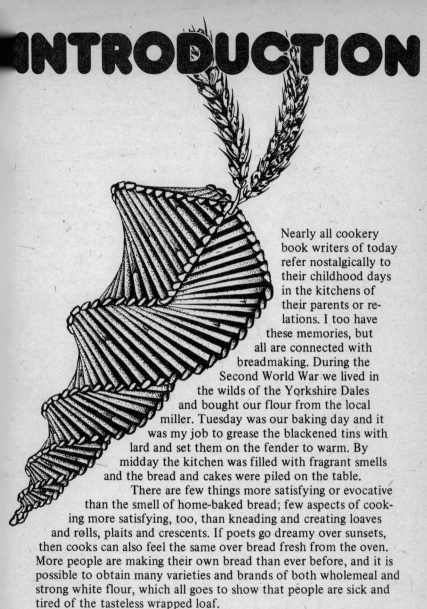

Nearly all cookery book writers of today refer nostalgically to their childhood days in the kitchens of their parents or relations. I too have these memories, but all are connected with breadmaking. During the Second World War we lived in the wilds of the Yorkshire Dales and bought our flour from the local miller. Tuesday was our baking day and it was my job to grease the blackened tins with lard and set them on the fender to warm. By midday the kitchen was filled with fragrant smells and the bread and cakes were piled on the table.

There are few things more satisfying or evocative than the smell of home-baked bread; few aspects of cooking more satisfying, too, than kneading and creating loaves and rolls, plaits and crescents. If poets go dreamy over sunsets, then cooks can also feel the same over bread fresh from the oven. More people are making their own bread than ever before, and it is possible to obtain many varieties and brands of both wholemeal and strong white flour, which all goes to show that people are sick and tired of the tasteless wrapped loaf.

Breadmaking is an age-old craft. History tells us that bread was worshipped by the Ancient Greeks, reverence being paid to Demeter, the goddess of cereals. Breadmaking scenes are depicted on Egyptian tombs and there are numerous Biblical references to bread. It has

7

always been 'the staff of life'. Originally, wheat was the cereal mostly used, followed by millet and barley. Modern wheats are constantly changing, and new and better varieties are being grown for both breads and cakes.

The venerable art of breadmaking should certainly not be avoided as something difficult or mysterious. Bread can be made during the course of your usual daily homemaking. The dough can be set by day or night to suit your own convenience. Successful breadmaking simply lies in the understanding of the qualities and characteristics of the few essential ingredien

I have attempted in this book to do tw things. First, to introduce to the practice of breadmaking those cooks who have been reluctant to try their hands at this satisfying art. Secondly, to encourage the unadventurous breadmaker to try recipes other than for the common white and brown loaf. I have therefore included a a variety of recipes for savoury breads and teabreads, most of which I had fun creating myself.

All the recipes have been well tried by me. They are divided into three grades: easy, moderately difficult, and for the experienced only. I have endeavoured to provide all the information necessary for success without, I hope, unnecessary verbiage or unwarranted assumptions concerning the reader's abilities—or lack of them.

Patricia Jacobs
1975

RECIPE GUIDE

Wholemeal Breads and Rolls

†recipe created by the author

White Breads and Rolls

†recipe created by the author

Tea Breads and Buns

†*recipe created by the author*

WEIGHTS AND MEASURES

All weights and measures are given in Imperial, Metric and American units.

> Metric = M
>
> American = A
>
> American cup measurements = C

OVEN TEMPERATURES

Oven temperatures are given in Fahrenheit (F), Centigrade (C), and the equivalent Gas Mark No.

ABBREVIATIONS

Throughout this book
tsp = teaspoon
table = tablespoon
dessert = dessertspoon

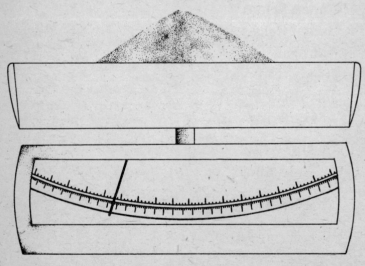

INGREDIENTS OF BREADMAKING

Yeast is a living plant which grows by budding when provided with suitable food and external conditions: air, warmth and moisture are essential contributory factors. Yeast can be fresh or dried and bought in health food stores or from bakers. Fresh yeast keeps perfectly well in a screw-topped jar in the refrigerator for two weeks. Fresh yeast cells digest the natural sugar content in the recipe ingredients and break it down into carbon dioxide, which causes the dough to rise. Dried yeast comes in tins or sachets, and it has to be dissolved in warm water or milk with one teaspoonful of sugar to render it usable. Sugar helps the growth of yeast, but too much makes the yeast cells shrink, likewise too much salt. The best temperature is between 80°F (27°C) and 85°F (29°C) and it is a help to keep bread tins warm before the dough is put into them. Where recipes call for fresh yeast and only dry is available, use half the quantity of dried to fresh.

Yeast measurements can be very confusing and often vague. Recipes refer to sachets and cubes, stating no quantity. The following notes will, I hope, help to clear up some of the doubts in peoples' minds.

Metric	American	Imperial
7 gm	2 heaped tsp	1½ heaped tsp or ¼ oz dried
15 gm	3¾ tsp	3 heaped tsp or ½ oz dried
15 gm	¾ cake or 1 package	½ oz fresh
30 gm	1½ cakes or 2 packages	1 oz fresh
55 gm	3 cakes	2 oz fresh
	or 2½ table	or 2 level table dried

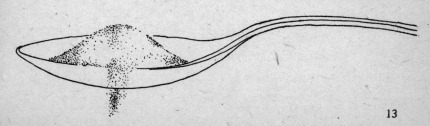

Flours

Strong White
The correct flour for white bread. Wheat before it is made into flour is either hard or soft. Hard wheat as used in strong flour is rich in protein and is more suitable for breadmaking because it has a high gluten content, which gives body and nutritional value to the loaf.

Cake Flours
These are sifted fine and made from soft wheat and are suitable for tea breads. Freshly milled white flour is pale yellow but becomes white after a short time. To speed this process most mills use a chemical agent which is rigourously controlled by the Government. Vitamin content lost in this process is replaced.

Wholemeal and Wholewheat
100% contains the whole of the wheat grain and is carefully stoneground so that nutrients and flavour are retained. It is completely free from chemicals and additives.

Farmhouse
Containing 81% of the wheat, it is lighter in colour and texture, but is also stoneground. Ideal for pastry and biscuits.

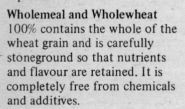

Rye

This is milled in three grades: fine, medium and coarse. Rye lacks the necessary protein for the formation of gluten and it is combined with wheat flour to give a less heavy, close-textured loaf. It is rich in nitrogen and produces a darker loaf than wheat flour.

Soya

Also lacks gluten forming protein and needs to be combined with other flours.

Granary

Contains malt and crushed wheat, giving it a rough, crunchy texture.

Scofa Scone Meal

This is excellent for soda bread and scones. As it is a blend of ingredients and already contains a raising agent, use the recipe given on the bag.

Gluten Flour

A high quality flour which is ideal for diets where starch intake must be low. It is wheat flour with the starch removed. Use as ordinary white flour.

Gluten Powder

This is sold in health food stores. It can be added to compost grown flours, which are low in gluten, and will give added bulk and lightness. Instructions are on the packet.

Additional Ingredients

Sugar to start the yeast working—White for white flour and Brown for brown flour.

Molasses gives colour and flavour to brown bread. It also contains concentrated vitamins.

Salt: Sea salt gives the best flavour. Grind straight from the salt mill into the flour.

Fats: These can include butter, vegetarian fats, lard or cooking oil. 1 oz (M 30gm, A 2 table) of fat is equivalent to 1 table oil (M 1 table, A 1¼ table).

Liquids: Water is the most usual liquid used. Skim milk or whole milk give added food value. Sour milk is good for soda bread. Potato water, i.e. the water in which potatoes have been cooked, gives a special flavour to white bread and improves the keeping quality. All liquids should be warm when added to the flour.

Fruit: Almost any dried fruit can be chopped up and added, usually after the first rising so as not to slow down the yeast action.

Seeds of carraway for rye bread and ground cardamom for continental plaits and sweet breads.

Sourdough Paste gives the traditional sour flavour to rye bread.

Nuts: Walnuts are the most successful. A pinch of curry powder in addition brings out the walnut flavour.

Crushed Wheat can be purchased from some bakers and health food stores. If you want to prepare your own to ensure freshness, buy a pound or so from a miller or corn chandler and grind a little in a coffee grinder or liquidizer.

Apart from sprinkling it on top of the bread, I add a handful or so to the bulk dough to improve the flavour and texture of the bread, and then add a little extra liquid.

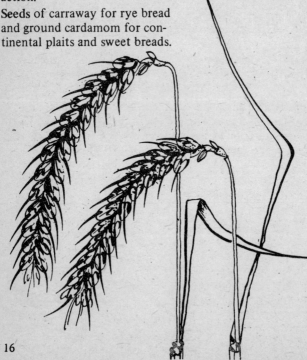

SHAPES AND TINS

Dough can be kneaded into a variety of shapes without a shaped tin. By using a baking sheet, dough can be shaped into larger knots, cottage loaves and plaits. The baking sheets supplied with the average oven are pretty small; one can, however, buy large enamel baking trays in kitchen equipment shops which specialise in tins for commercial bakers. Providing your oven is large enough, it is possible to make long batons and plaits.

By using standard **cake and loaf tins** and **Continental ring moulds**, the dough can be swiftly and easily pressed into the tins and will result in attractively shaped loaves and tea breads.

Rolls can be made into a variety of shapes, the easiest method being to break off small pieces of dough, roll them under the hands into long strands and knot loosely.

Dough can be rolled out like pastry and cut with a glass or scone cutter, and rolls can then be placed close together on the baking sheet. Thus they keep nice and moist and can be separated when ready to use.

Small china soufflé dishes make attractive 'dolly' moulds for children, likewise the tiny square bread tins to be found in some cookshops.

Flower pots make ideal and attractive moulds for bread. The clay retains the heat in the same way as the old brick bakers' ovens. The texture of the crust is crunchy also. It is important, however, to season the pots first by larding or oiling them well and baking in a very hot oven at 450°F (230°C, Gas Mark 8) on two occasions before you actually want to use them. **Large coffee or fruit juice tins** are useful for sausage shaped loaves, provided they are well greased.

Farmhouse: This is the best shape to use if sandwiches are needed. It represents the square conventional loaf traditionally baked on the farm.

Shape by rolling the dough swiss roll fashion. Make three gashes on the top—a double-sided razor blade does this more effectively than a knife, which tends to pull and distort the dough.

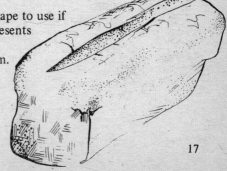

Cottage: I think this is everybody's favourite. It conjures up cosy cottage baking days, the cat curled up on the fender and a pile of glossy cottage loaves on the well scrubbed table! This is one of the oldest English bread shapes. Divide the dough into two pieces, one piece larger than the other. Shape into two rounds, and place the smaller on top. Make a hole through the middle of both pieces with the floured handle of a spoon.

The Plait: This is a universal bread shape, lending itself to Harvest Thanksgiving loaves and Continental sugar glazed confections. The plait can be either a two or a three strand loaf.

Plait 1: Shape the dough into an oblong with a fat middle, tapering off the ends. Using a sharp knife or kitchen scissors, cut up the middle of the dough leaving the top couple of inches joined.

Plait loosely and seal the ends with water. Turn the plait over and place on a floured baking sheet.

Plait 2: Roll the dough into an oblong with a rolling pin. Cut into three even pieces lengthways. Roll each under the hand as evenly as possible, join the three strands of dough together and moisten with water. Plait as above.

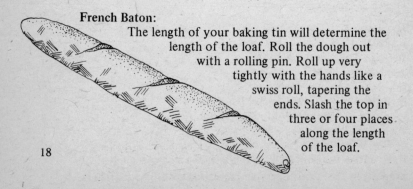

French Baton:
The length of your baking tin will determine the length of the loaf. Roll the dough out with a rolling pin. Roll up very tightly with the hands like a swiss roll, tapering the ends. Slash the top in three or four places along the length of the loaf.

Crown Loaf: Either a sweet or a plain dough can be used for this shape. It can be a table centre for a dinner party, each guest pulling their own roll from the crown. If your oven is a small one, space can be saved by baking fourteen rolls in two tins.

Using 1 lb (M 450gm, A 4 C) of dough, divide into seven balls. Roll under the hands and aim to make all the rolls the same size. Place six balls in a greased Victoria sandwich tin and put the seventh ball in the centre.

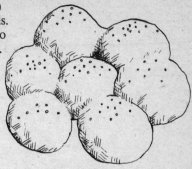

The Cob: This shape resembles the nut of the same name. Brown flour should always be used, with a generous scattering of crushed wheat overall. The cob can be baked in a sandwich tin, or on a tin plate if a baking sheet is not available.

Work the dough into a ball by pulling the edges into the centre in a continuous circular movement. Finish off by spinning the ball of dough between the palms.

Tin Loaf:
The loaves take the shape of the tin in which they are baked, but it is necessary to shape the dough correctly before pressing it into the tin.

Take an oblong piece of dough, flatten with the side of the hand and roll up tightly, drop into the tin, pressing down into the corners if the tin is a rectangular one. Tin sizes vary, but as long as the dough only half fills the tin at the start, there is room for the doubling of the volume which takes place in proving and baking.
Keep a look out for the **mini tins** which can provide delightful presents in the form of sample loaves for enthusiastic friends.

KNEADING

The importance of kneading cannot be over-emphasised. If the dough is insufficiently worked, the bread will be like a rock, close textured and heavy!

Kneading distributes the yeast evenly in the dough, incorporating air and helping the yeast to continue its work. During the process of kneading, the dough will change its texture, becoming smoother and silkier. If you have an electric mixer, the dough hook will do the job for you, but it will not be so satisfying as kneading the dough by hand and *feeling* it change.

The first stage of kneading can be done in a mixing bowl, which should always be a large and roomy one. When the flour has absorbed all the liquid, gather together the ball of dough in the right hand, pulling the edges into the centre with the fingers and pressing down with the heel of the hand. The left hand is turning the bowl slowly to the right. You will find that with a little practice this movement soon becomes a natural and easy one. After five minutes or so of kneading in the bowl, turn the dough out onto a floured board or work top. A cool slab of marble may be ideal for pastry, but I prefer a large square of wood to work on. Continue to use the circular movement working from the outside in, using both hands if it is easier.

A wholemeal dough will take more time to become smooth than a white dough which has more fat and liquid in it. A dough which is initially too slack and soft will have to be beaten with the hand, which should be well floured. Take a handful of the dough and bang it down hard on the board. After a time it will change its texture and become more manageable. The dough hook has the advantage over the hands here because it enables very slack doughs to be worked more easily.

Watchpoint: If the dough is over-moist while still in the bowl, turn it out onto a floured board and knead in extra flour. If the dough is too dry, don't turn it out of the basin until you have added sufficient liquid to make it the right consistency, as it is impossible to add liquid at a later stage.

RISING

This is the most important stage after kneading. Rising the dough can be carried out in several ways to suit your convenience. One should never be a slave to the dough! Make it work for you the way you want it to, fitting the daily tasks in between stages of bread-making. Don't worry about cold draughts killing the yeast either. The slower the rise the more even textured will be the finished product.

Refrigerator Rising
Place the dough in a bowl allowing room for rising. Cover with foil.
Doughs mixed with water will keep for three days.
Doughs high in fat will keep for a week.
Milk dough will keep for four days.
When ready to use, turn the dough out of the chilled bowl onto a board and allow it to return to room temperature before proceeding to shape.

Overnight Rising in a cool larder.
Place in a large oiled saucepan with a lid or in a mixing bowl and wrap in polythene. A plastic pillowcase size bag is ideal. Next morning use the dough as after refrigerator rising.

Room Temperature Rising
Place the dough in an oiled plastic bag. The dough breathes inside the closed polythene bag and keeps moist. It can also be left in the bowl and placed inside a closed polythene bag. If the dough is a slack one and adheres to the bag when it is slipped out, leave the dough to dry, after which it can be brushed off the bag.
Allow one-and-a-half to two hours rising in this temperature.

Airing Cupboard Rising, or similar place, requires one hour.
Procedure is the same as with the room temperature method.

Knocking Back
During the process of rising, the dough becomes filled with gas, and it must therefore be knocked back otherwise the finished loaf will be unevenly textured and full of holes. Tip the dough out of its rising receptacle onto a floured board, roll up like a Swiss roll twice, pressing down hard as you do so. The dough will feel silky and air bubbles may appear which is a good sign.

PROVING

This is another word for the second rising which must take place after the dough has been 'knocked back'. It needs a chance to recover after it has been shaped and before it is put into the oven. In some parts of Britain the term 'setting' is used.

This can be considered the last lap in the preparation of the dough. Proving is carried out inside a closed polythene bag, again small ones for bread tins and large ones for baking sheets.

The room temperature should be warm.
Rolls will take twenty to thirty minutes.
Dough proving in a tin will take longer to rise than dough without a tin, i.e. cobs or plaits.

Loaves which are under-proved will be close-textured and have 'fly-away' tops. Thirty to forty minutes proving time should be allowed. Ideally, the tins should be filled 2/3rds full and the remining 1/3rd will be taken up in proving. The ready-proved loaf should be soft and puffy. Doughs do vary in their ability to rise according to the ingredients used.

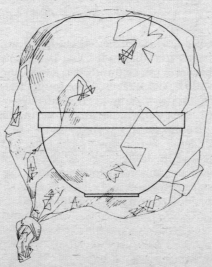

BAKING

When the 'proving' dough reaches the top of the tins, it is ready to be glazed and/or sprinkled with seeds and put in the very hot oven.

Between 400°F (200°C, Gas Mark 6) and 425°F (220°C, Gas Mark 7) is the ideal baking temperature for bread. Most electric ovens need thirty minutes to reach this setting. Meanwhile, the bread is proving on the top of the cooker which produces a gentle, gradual warmth. Too hot an oven is a better fault than one not hot enough!

Rolls will be cooked in twenty minutes, but loaves will need forty minutes or longer, according to the size. During the last twenty minutes, the loaves can be turned in the oven and the heat reduced to 375°F (190°C, Gas Mark 5). I like to slip loaves out of their tins during the last five minutes to crisp the sides and bottoms.

A shallow tin of boiling water in the base of the oven helps to produce a crisper crust. Likewise, spraying with water at ten minute intervals. Modern bakery ovens are steam injected, and are therefore able to achieve the really hard crusts on the outside.

Always bake loaves and rolls in the top part of the oven. When baked, remove from the oven and cool on a wire rack.

Most breads and rolls freeze well if securely sealed in polythene bags.

FINISHES AND TOPPINGS FOR BREAD

To give an attractive-looking and tasty finish to your bread, use the appropriate glaze or topping as suggested below, or as directed in the recipes following in this book.

Glaze
- with salty water for a crisp crust on brown and white breads
- with whole egg beaten for white rolls
- with cream or milk for both white rolls and milk breads
- with beaten egg yolk and top of the milk for a rich, glossy finish on tea breads
- with warmed honey or sugar syrup for a sweeter tasting topping on tea breads

Glaze recipes

Salt and water glaze for brown and white bread. Add 1tsp salt (M 1 tsp, A 1¼ tsp) to ¼ pint (M 140ml, A¾ C) water. Using a small plastic squeezy spray bottle, spray the loaves both before and during baking with salty water to achieve a crisp crust. Spray the tins as well for all rolls and croissants. The steam will produce a good rise. A tin of boiling water in the base of the oven will supply steam to make extra crusty bread.

Egg white and sugar glaze is good for the French baton type of loaf
Use 1 tsp (M 1 tsp, A 1¼ tsp) water to each egg white
Beat lightly and paint loaves at the start of baking.

Sugar Glaze for tea buns
4 oz (M 115 gm, A 1 C) granulated sugar
6 table milk (M 6 table, A 7½ table)
Dissolve the sugar in the milk and boil for three minutes. Store in
a Kilner jar in the refrigerator if not needed immediately.

Honey Glaze for tea breads
1 tsp (M 1 tsp, A 1¼ tsp) liquid honey mixed and warmed with
1 tsp (M 1 tsp, A 1¼ tsp) milk.

Sprinkle with poppy seeds, sesame, crushed wheat or rolled oats,
depending on the
bread you are
making. Use
crushed coffee
sugar for buns
and some tea
breads.

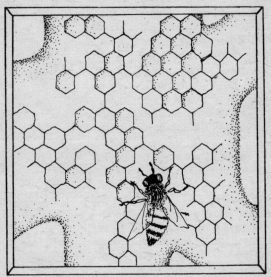

Wholemeal Breads and Rolls

Herb Soda Loaf*

RECIPE CREATED BY THE AUTHOR*

The perfect picnic bread. Use for savoury sandwiches filled with garlic butter and tomato slices. As this is a fatless bread, it is best eaten the day it is made.

1 Flat Cake

Ingredients

1 lb (M 450 gm, A 4 C) plain white flour *or* brown wholewheat

1 tsp (M 1 tsp, A 1¼ tsp) salt

2 tsp (M 2 tsp, A 2½ tsp) bicarbonate of soda

2 tsp (M 2 tsp, A 2½ tsp) cream of tartar

8 fl.oz (M 225 ml, A 1 C) warm sour milk

2 table (M 2 table, A 2½ table) freshly cut herbs, such as mint, parsley, chives, sage and fennel, chopped in a parsley mill.

Method

1. Place all the dry ingredients in a bowl.

2. Make a well and pour in the warm sour milk to give a soft dough. Add extra warm sour milk if necessary.

3. Shape with floured hands on a well dredged board into a round flat cake.

4. Bake at once on a floured sheet at 400°F (200°C, Gas Mark 6) for 40 minutes.

5. For a change, try using small spoonfuls of the dough to make mini-rolls.

GRANARY LOAF*

Granary flour contains malted wheat, rye and wheatmeal. It produces a pleasant, nutty-flavoured loaf. A good all-purpose bread for any meal.

2 Cobs

Ingredients

1½lb (M 675 gm, A 6 C) granary flour

1½ tsp (M 1½ tsp, A 2 tsp) corn oil

1 dessert (M 1 dessert, A 1¼ dessert) salt

½oz (M 15 gm, A 3 tsp) dried yeast

¾ pint (M 425 ml, A 2 C) warm water

1 dessert (M 1 dessert, A 1¼ dessert) molasses

Method

1. Put the yeast into a cup with enough warm water to cover, and leave for 10 minutes.
2. Dissolve the molasses in the rest of the water and add the oil.
3. Make a well in the flour in the mixing bowl and add the rest of the ingredients.
4. Mix and knead thoroughly.
5. Rise for 1 hour inside a closed polythene bag.
6. Take out and divide into two round cobs. Place in floured tins.
7. Prove for 30 minutes.
8. Paint with beaten egg or milk and bake at 400°F (200°C, Gas Mark 6) for 30 to 40 minutes.

SOYA ROLLS*

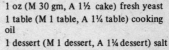
RECIPE CREATED BY THE AUTHOR

The small quantity of soya flour in this recipe is a good nutritional addition. The rolls are better if baked until they only have a light crust. All rolls which are intended to be reheated should be slightly under-baked to allow for this. As with all soya breads, these rolls are a complement to most foods.

15 Knotted Rolls

Ingredients

1 lb (M 450 gm, A 3½ C) wholemeal flour

8 oz (M 225 gm, A 2 C) strong white flour

4 oz (M 115 gm, A 1 C) soya flour

1 oz (M 30 gm, A 1½ cake) fresh yeast

1 table (M 1 table, A 1¼ table) cooking oil

1 dessert (M 1 dessert, A 1¼ dessert) salt

¾ pint (M 425 ml, A 2 C) warm skim milk

Method

1. Put all the flours into a large bowl.
2. Dissolve the yeast in a little of the warm skim milk and leave for 5 minutes to froth.
3. Make a well in the flour and pour in the yeast liquid and remaining milk.
4. Add the oil and mix well. Knead until smooth.
5. Rise inside a closed polythene bag until doubled in bulk—approximately one hour.
6. Knock back and leave another hour. Take out and place on a floured board.
7. Divide into 15 balls. Roll under the hands into knots (see 'Shapes' on page 17).
8. Place the rolls on a flat floured tin and prove in a closed polythene bag for 20 minutes.
9. Glaze with beaten egg or spray with water and bake at 425°F (200°C, Gas Mark 7) for 30 minutes.

FLOUR

YEAST

CARAWAY SE

1975

Wholemeal Bread*

This is the basic brown loaf. Brown bread tends to dry out, and I find that it keeps better if it is baked in small rather than large tins. As this recipe contains all brown flour and no white, it is a very substantial and satisfying loaf.

2 Large or 4 Small Loaves

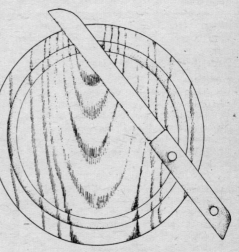

Ingredients

2½ lb (M 1¼ kg, A 8¾ C) 100% stone-ground wholemeal flour

2 tsp (M 2 tsp, A 2½ tsp) sea salt

2 oz (M 55 gm, A 4 table) any cooking fat

1 oz (M 30 gm, A 1½ cake) fresh yeast

1 dessert (M 1 dessert, A 1¼ dessert) molasses

1 small handful of crushed wheat

1¼ pints (M 625 ml, A 3 C) warm water. The amount of water required varies with the absorbency of the flour. Add extra if needed.

Method

1. Put the flour and salt into a large bowl and make a well in the centre.
2. Put the yeast into a small bowl, add ¼ pint (M 140 ml, A ¾ C) warm water, leave to froth.
3. Stir the molasses into the remaining water.
4. Melt the fat and cool.
5. Pour all the liquids into the well and mix thoroughly. Knead, adding additional water if required, to obtain a putty-like dough.
6. Rise by placing the bowl inside a closed polythene bag for 1½-2 hours until the dough has doubled in size. Brown flour is slower to rise than white.
7. Turn out of the bowl onto a floured board, knead lightly, shaping the dough into oblongs, rolling them by hand and tucking them into well-greased tins, seam side down.
8. Prove inside a closed polythene bag for 20-30 minutes.
9. Brush with water and sprinkle thickly with crushed wheat.
10. Bake at 425°F (220°C, Gas Mark 7) for 20 minutes, then turn loaves round and the oven down to 400°F (200°C, Gas Mark 6) for a further 20 minutes.

Light Wholemeal Bread*

A lighter textured loaf can be made by using half wholemeal and half white flour.

2 Large or 4 Small Loaves

Ingredients

1 lb (M 450 gm, A 3½ C) 100% wholemeal flour

1½ lb (M 675 gm, A 6 C) strong white flour

1 oz (M 30 gm, A 1½ cake) fresh yeast

2 table (M 2 table, A 2¼ table) cooking oil

2 tsp (M 2 tsp, A 2½ tsp) sea salt

1 heaped tsp (M 1 tsp, A 1¼ heaped tsp) molasses

1½ pints (M ¾ litre, A 3¾ C) warm milk and water, mixed

Method

Proceed as for wholemeal recipe.

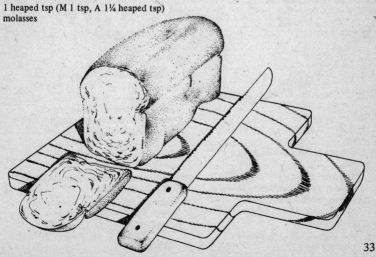

WHOLEWHEAT SESAME ROLLS*

These are tasty, all-purpose rolls, equally good with either sweet or savoury foods.

3 Dozen Rolls

Ingredients

1 lb (M 450 gm, A 3½ C) whole-meal flour

1½ lb (M 675 gm, A 6 C) strong white flour

1 oz (M 30 gm, A 1½ cake) fresh yeast

2 oz (M 55 gm, A 4 table) margarine—melted

1 dessert (M 1 dessert, A 1¼ dessert) salt

1½ pints (M 850 ml, A 3¾ C) warm water approximately

1 dessert (M 1 dessert, A 1¼ dessert) sesame seeds

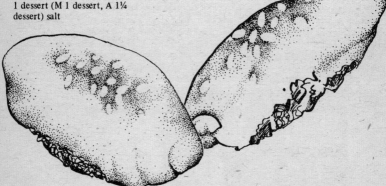

Method

1. Mix the flours together in a large bowl and add salt and sesame seeds.
2. Cream yeast with 8 fl oz (225 gm, A 1 C) of warm water and wait until it starts working, then add to the flour.
3. Add the melted margarine and water by degrees.
4. Knead well.
5. Rise inside a closed polythene bag until doubled in size.
6. Roll into a long rope and cut off sections with a sharp knife.
7. Shape into oblongs. Press out flat with the side of the hand and roll up tightly. Place seam side down on a floured sheet.
8. Prove inside a closed polythene bag for 20-30 minutes.
9. Spray with water and sprinkle each roll with more sesame seeds.
10. Bake at 400°F (200°C, Gas Mark 6) for 25 minutes. The longer they cook, the crustier they will be.

34

WHOLEMEAL SODA BREAD*

All soda breads are better eaten the day of baking. Delicious for tea with a good homemade jam; equally good eaten with a slab of Cheddar cheese and pickled onions.

To preserve the moistness of a soda loaf, keep in a plastic lidded box in the fridge. Soda bread should not be toasted as the texture is too crumbly.

2 Flat Cakes

Ingredients

1 lb 8oz (M 675 gm, A 6 C) 100% wholemeal flour

8 oz (M 225 gm, A 2 C) strong white flour

2 tsp (M 2 tsp, A 2½ tsp) brown sugar

1 oz (M 30 gm, A 2 table) baking powder

2 oz (M 55 gm, A ¼ C) margarine –melted

2 table (M 2 table, A 2¼ table) plain yoghurt

1 pint (M ½ litre, A 2½ C) warm sour milk

Method

1. Mix dry ingredients and place in bowl.
2. Work melted margarine into flour.
3. Add milk and mix carefully and thoroughly. This dough is a sticky one.
4. Shape with floured hands into two flat round shapes.
5. Place on floured baking sheet and brush with milk.
6. Bake in a hot oven 400°F (200°C, Gas Mark 6) for about 40 minutes.

    No rising, knocking back or proving is necessary as there is no yeast used in this recipe.

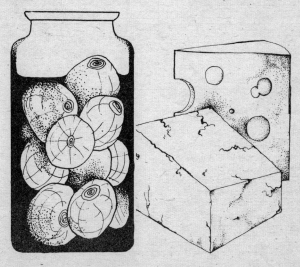

BLACK BREAD**

This bread is delicious with soups. It is also a good party bread because its flavour offsets the harshness of strong spirit drinks, and it makes a tasty base for open sandwiches. It is sometimes difficult to obtain the dark rye flour used in this recipe, but a lighter flour can be substituted—although the finished loaf will then also be lighter. This loaf does not resemble the traditional German black bread or pumpernickel, which is usually made from unbolted rye flour, very dark in colour and rough textured.

2 Long Loaves

Ingredients
1½ lb (M 675 gm, A 5¼ C) dark rye flour

1 oz (M 30 gm, A 1½ cake) fresh yeast

1 tsp (M 1 tsp, A 1¼ tsp) salt

1 pint (M ½ litre, A 2½ C) warm milk

1 table (M 1 table, A 1¼ table) molasses

½ tsp (M ½ tsp, A ½ tsp) carraway seeds

Method

1. Dissolve the yeast in a ¼ of the warm milk.

2. Put 1/3 of the flour into a roomy bowl, make a well and pour in the yeast.

3. Draw the flour over the well until the yeast is covered and leave this to rise until the yeast bubbles through and the mixture is frothy.

4. Stir the molasses and salt into the rest of the warm milk.

5. Add the remaining flour and liquids to the basin. Mix and knead well.

6. Rise inside a closed polythene bag until doubled in size.

7. Divide the dough into two pieces and shape into long loaves.

8. Prove inside a closed polythene bag for 15 minutes.

9. Brush with milk, sprinkle with seeds and bake at 400°F (200°C, Gas Mark 6) for 60 minutes or until firm and crusty on the base.

BOSTON BREAD**

A traditional American steamed
savoury bread, which is eaten warm
and fresh for breakfast with baked
beans or griddle cakes. It is the only
bread I know which is cut with a piece
of taut string to prevent it from crumbling!

4 Round Loaves

Ingredients

4 oz (M 115 gm, A 1 C) strong white flour
4 oz (M 115 gm, A 1 C) cornmeal or semolina
4 oz (M 115 gm, A 1 C) wholemeal flour
1 tsp (M 1 tsp, A 1¼ tsp) baking powder
1 tsp (M 1 tsp, A 1¼ tsp) salt
1 tsp (M 1 tsp, A 1¼ tsp) bicarbonate of soda
3 table (M 3 table, A 3¾ table) molasses
8 fl oz (M ¼ litre, A 1 C) natural yoghurt or buttermilk
(warmed)
8 fl oz (M ¼ litre, A 1 C) skim milk (warmed)

Method

1. Put all dry ingredients into a bowl.
2. Beat together the milk, molasses and yoghurt.
3. Pour into the dry ingredients and mix well.
4. Have ready 4 large greased and floured vegetable or
   fruit juice cans (baked bean cans are ideal) and fill
   with the mixture.
5. Cover the tops with foil.
6. Place on a trivet and put in a roomy saucepan.
7. Pour in boiling water to 1 inch depth. Cover with a
   lid and steam 3 hours, adding extra water.
8. Remove the cans from the water and take off foil.
9. Place the cans in a hot oven 450°F (230°C, Gas Mark 8)
   to dry off for 5 minutes.
10. Leave to cool before removing from the cans.

37

BUCKWHEAT BREAD**

RECIPE CREATED BY THE AUTHOR

This is a moist bread, full of flavour. The generous quantity of yeast used makes a light loaf which is at its best when eaten with a strong cheese such as Lancashire. Make this recipe in the blender and mixer.

3 Small Loaves

Ingredients

12 oz (M 350 gm, A 2¾ C) 100% wholemeal flour

½ oz (M 15 gm, A 1 tsp) salt

8 oz (M 225 gm, A 1¾ C) buckwheat flour

5 oz (M 140 gm, A 1¼ C) strong white flour

1 dessert (M 1 dessert, A 1¼ dessert) molasses

2 oz (M 55 gm, A 3 cake) fresh yeast

12 fl oz (M 425 ml, A 1½ C) warm water

2 table (M 2 table, A 2½ table) cooking oil

1 oz (M 30 gm, A ½ table) lard

Method

1. Pour 8 fl oz (M 225 gm, A 1 C) of warm water into the blender, add yeast and molasses.
2. Leave for 5 minutes.
3. Blend for 15 seconds.
4. Add oil and blend for 5 seconds.
5. Put all the dry ingredients into the mixer bowl, make a well in the middle and pour in the yeast mixture.
6. Melt the lard and add.
7. Knead with the dough hook until the dough forms a compact ball, adding the remaining 4 fl oz (M 112 gm, A ½ C) of liquid to make a putty-like dough. Brands of flour vary, and not all the warm water may be needed.
8. Put to rise in a closed polythene bag for approximately 1 hour and 40 minutes at warm room temperature.
9. Knock back and shape into 3 loaves.
10. Prove in the tins in a closed polythene bag for 30-40 minutes.
11. Bake at 400°F (200°C, Gas Mark 6) for 30 minutes.

FLOWER POT WHOLEWHEAT LOAVES**

The flower pots must be seasoned first*. This is most important. Pots measuring 4" (M 10 cm) across are the most sensible to use as they bake quickly.

The dough is made up of equal proportions of white and brown flour and is lighter in texture than when all wholemeal is used. The shape is very attractive and cuts into neat rounds.

4 Pots

Ingredients

1 lb (M 450 gm, A 3½ C) 100% stoneground wholemeal flour

4 tsp (M 4 tsp, A 5 tsp) sea salt

1 lb (M 450 gm, A 4 C) strong white flour

20 fl oz (M ½ litre, A 2½ C) warm water with 1 dessert (M 1 dessert, A 1¼ dessert) molasses stirred into it

1 oz (M 30 gm, A 1½ cake) fresh yeast

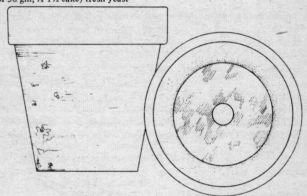

Method

1. Put the flours into a bowl and make a well.

2. Dissolve the yeast in a cup of the liquid and leave to froth.

3. Add the molasses to the water and stir until dissolved.

4. Pour the liquids into the well and mix.

5. Knead until smooth, adding a little extra liquid if necessary.

6. Rise inside a closed polythene bag until doubled in bulk—1 hour approx.

7. Knock back the dough and divide into 4 pieces.

8. Shape into balls and press into the prepared pots.

9. Snip the tops with kitchen scissors and prove inside a closed polythene bag for 20 minutes.

10. Bake in a hot oven 450°F (230°C, Gas Mark 8) for 30 minutes. After 15 minutes spray the loaves with salty water. When almost baked, remove the pots and finish off the loaves in the hot oven until crusty outside.

*See 'Shapes' on page 17

39

RECIPE CREATED BY THE AUTHOR

HEALTH BREAD**

A close-textured loaf, highly nutritious and satisfying. It is not suitable for forming into rolls. Delicious with any cheese, but even better eaten with unsalted butter alone.

2 Small Loaves

Ingredients

1 lb (M 450 gm, A 3½ C) 100% wholemeal flour

1 tsp (M 1 tsp, A 1¼ tsp) sea salt

1 oz (M 30 gm, A ¼ C) All Bran

1½ tsp (M 1½ tsp, A 2 tsp) dried yeast

2 table (M 2 table, A 2½ table) liquid honey

2 table (M 2 table, A 2½ table) crunchy peanut butter

¾ pint (M 425 ml, A 2 C) warm water

Method

1. Dissolve yeast in a little of the warm water.
2. Warm honey and peanut butter in rest of water.
3. Put dry ingredients into mixing bowl.
4. Make a well in the middle and pour in all the liquids.
5. Mix and knead well.
6. Rise for 1 hour or until doubled in bulk, inside a closed polythene bag.
   No proving is necessary.
7. Press into 2 small loaf tins.
8. Glaze with beaten egg.
9. Bake at 400°F (200°C, Gas Mark 6) for 15 minutes and at 350°F (180°C, Gas Mark 4) for a further 15 minutes.

MOLASSES AND RYE COBS**

The blend of flours and molasses gives this bread an unusual texture and flavour. The cobs can be rolled in crushed wheat before they are set for the final rising, to give an added crunchy finish. Delectable if allowed to rest for a day, foil wrapped in the fridge, then cut thin, spread with cream cheese and broken walnuts, and made into sandwiches.

4 Small Loaves

Ingredients

2 lb (M 900 gm, A 8 C) strong flour

1 oz (M 30 gm, A 1½ cake) fresh yeast

1 lb (M 450 gm, A 3½ C) coarse rye flour

1 pint (M ½ litre, A 2½ C) skimmed milk, made with powder and warm water

4 tsp (M 4 tsp, A 5 tsp) salt

4 table (M 4 table, A 5 table) blackstrap molasses

4 table (M 4 table, A 5 table) cooking oil

½ pint (M ¼ litre, A 1¼ C) warm water

2 table (M 2 table, A 2½ table) carraway seeds

Method

1. Dissolve yeast in ½ pint (M ¼ litre, A 1¼ C) warm water. Leave until frothy.

2. Stir molasses, oil, seeds, milk and yeast liquid into the white flour in a mixing bowl.

3. Add rye flour. Mix and knead. The dough is a soft one.

4. Rise inside a closed polythene bag for 1½-2 hours.

5. Shape into 4 round cakes and press into 6" sandwich tins or simply place on a baking sheet.

6. Prove inside a closed polythene bag for 30 minutes.

7. Spray with water and bake at 375°F (190°C, Gas Mark 5) for 40 minutes.

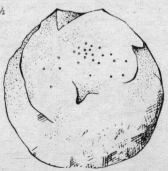

SICILIAN BREAD**

I prefer to bake this bread without a tin; the crustiness makes it more flavoursome. The recipe is an adaptation of Sicilian unleavened bread. It is a delicious bread, both filling and highly nutritious, and the ideal companion to a snack of olives, cheese and wine.

1 Loaf

Ingredients

10 oz (M 280 gm, A 2½ C) 100% wholewheat flour

3 table (M 3 table, A 3 ¾ table) wheat germ

3 table (M 3 table, A 3¾ table) soya flour

4 table (M 4 table, A 5 table) skim milk powder

2 tsp (M 2 tsp, A 2½ tsp) molasses

1 tsp (M 1 tsp, A 1¼ tsp) sea salt

½ oz (M 15 gm, A ¾ cake) fresh yeast

1 table (M 1 table, A 1¼ table) corn oil

½ pint (M ¼ litre, A 1¼ C) warm water

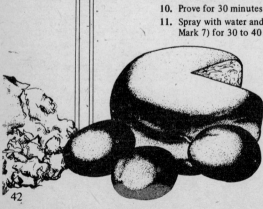

Method

1. Dissolve the yeast in the warm water.
2. Leave to froth.
3. Put all the dry ingredients in a bowl and make a well.
4. Drop in the molasses and oil and the yeast liquid.
5. Mix well. The dough is a compact, solid one.
6. Knead hard to distribute the yeast.
7. Rise in a closed polythene bag for approximately 1-2 hours or until doubled in size.
8. Knock back and leave for a further hour. This dough can be left overnight in the refrigerator, well covered.
9. Turn out onto a board and knead briefly, shaping into a loaf tin.
10. Prove for 30 minutes in a closed polythene bag.
11. Spray with water and bake at 425°F (220°C, Gas Mark 7) for 30 to 40 minutes.

SOYA SEMOLINA BREAD**

A soya loaf makes a pleasant change in both the baking programme and the diet. Soya flour has a mealy texture, and when it is combined with other flours the finished loaf is unique in flavour. This is a good bread to toast and eat with either cheese or homemade jam.

4 Cobs

Ingredients

8 oz (M 225 gm, A 1¾ C) 100% wholemeal flour

4 oz (M 115 gm, A 1 C) rye flour

6 oz (M 170 gm, A 1½ C) strong white flour

1 dessert (M 1 dessert, A 1¼ dessert) salt

4 oz (M 115 gm, A 1 C) semolina

3 oz (M 85 gm, A ¾ C) porridge oats

1 oz (M 30 gm, A 1½ cake) fresh yeast

2 table (M 2 table, A 2½ table) cooked soya beans

¾ pint (M 425 ml, A 2 C) warm water

2 table (M 2 table, A 2½ table) corn oil

1 table (M 1 table, A 1¼ table) honey

Method

1. Put the first five ingredients into a large bowl.

2. Cream the yeast with ¼ pint (M 140 ml, A ¾ C) warm water and leave for 5 minutes.

3. Add the honey and corn oil to remainder of the warm water and put in the goblet of the liquidizer with the soya beans. Liquidize until smooth.

4. Add yeast and contents of goblet to the flour and mix well.

5. Knead until smooth.

6. Rise inside a closed polythene bag for 1 - 1½ hours or until doubled in size.

7. Take out and shape into 4 cobs or use well greased bread tins.

8. Prove inside a closed polythene bag for 20 minutes.

9. Bake at 425°F (220°C, Gas Mark 7) for 30 to 40 minutes. Spray the loaves with salty water after the first 10 minutes and during the last 10 minutes of cooking.

RECIPE CREATED BY THE AUTHOR

SOYA WHOLEWHEAT BREAD**

A very nutritious and delicious loaf, which eats well with either sweet or savoury foods. The combination of beaten egg and corn oil ensures a moist, good-keeping bread. The wholewheat flour may be replaced by rye flour for a change.

2 Loaves

Ingredients

1 lb (M 450 gm, A 4 C) strong white flour

8 oz (M 225 gm, A 1¾ C) wholewheat flour

4 oz (M 115 gm, A 1 C) soya flour

2 tsp (M 2 tsp, A 2½ tsp) salt

4 oz (M 115 gm, A 1 C) rolled oats

2 oz (M 50 gm, A ½ C) wheat germ

2 fl oz (M 55 ml, A ¼ C) corn oil

1 beaten egg

2 dessert (M 2 dessert, A 2¼ dessert) soft brown sugar

1½ oz (M 45 gm, A 2¼ cake) fresh yeast

1 pint + 2 oz (M ½ litre + 55 ml, A 2½ C + ¾ C) warm skim milk

Method

1. Put all the dry ingredients into a bowl.
2. Cream yeast with 2 oz (M 55 ml, A ¾ C) liquid. Leave for 5 minutes.
3. Beat the egg and add corn oil to the rest of the liquid.
4. Pour liquids into flour and mix well.
5. Knead, adding extra white flour, if necessary
6. Rise inside a closed polythene bag for 1-1½ hours, or until doubled in bulk.
7. Knock back. Divide into two pieces.
8. Form into two round cobs.
9. Place on an oiled and floured baking sheet and prove inside a closed polythene bag for 25 minutes.
10. Spray with water and sprinkle with oats.
11. Bake at 425°F (220°C, Gas Mark 7) for 40 minutes.

Wholemeal Walnut Plaits**

This plait is at its best eaten with cheese and salad. The addition of a little curry powder to the ingredients gives a delicious, unusual taste. If kept in the bread bin for a day to mature, the walnut flavour will be stronger.

2 Large Plaits

Ingredients

2 lb (M 900 gm, A 7 C) "compost" 100% brown flour

1 lb (M 450 gm, A 4 C) strong white flour

2 tsp (M 2 tsp, A 2¼ tsp) curry powder

1 oz (M 30 gm, A 1½ cake) fresh yeast

1 table (M 1 table, A 1¼ table) salt

2 oz (M 55 gm, A ¼ C) lard or margarine

1 dessert (M 1 dessert, A 1¼ dessert) molasses

Small handful of crushed wheat

1½ pints (M ¾ litre, A 3¾ C) warm water

4 oz (M 115 gm, A 2/3 C) broken walnuts

Method

1. Dissolve the yeast in ½ pint (M ¼ litre, A 1¼ C) of warm water.

2. Add the molasses and stir well. Leave to froth up.

3. Melt the lard, cool and add to the yeast liquid.

4. Put the dry ingredients in a large bowl, pour in the yeast liquid and stir gradually incorporating the flour.

5. Add the remaining warm water.

6. Rise inside a closed polythene bag for 1 hour.

7. Divide into two pieces.

8. Roll out with a rolling pin on a floured board and sprinkle the surface with half the broken walnuts for each plait.

9. Roll lightly with the hands, Swiss-roll fashion.

10. Shape each into an oblong and plait*.

11. Prove in a closed polythene bag for 30 minutes.

12. Glaze with beaten egg and bake at 400°F (200°C, Gas Mark 6) for 40 minutes.

*See shapes on page 18.

45

LIGHT RYE BREAD***

RECIPE CREATED BY THE AUTHOR

3 Small Loaves

Rye breads differ from country to country, but all are based on the sourdough preparation. The finished loaf is close textured and heavier than the commercial rye loaf. It is particularly good for open sandwiches, having a firm texture to hold the toppings, and is less likely to go soggy. The carraway seeds are traditional and can be sprinkled on the proven loaf, or worked into the dough at the start of rising.

First prepare the sourdough with
2 oz (M 55 gm, A scant ½ C) 81% brown flour
3 oz (M 85 gm, A ¾ C) fine rye flour
¼ tsp (M ¼ tsp, A ½ tsp) dried yeast
3 oz (M 85 ml, A 7 table) warm water

Place the yeast in the water for 10 minutes, after which it will appear frothy. Then put the flour in a mixing bowl and add the yeast mixture. Rise inside a closed polythene bag placed in the airing cupboard for 24 hours.

Next day prepare the dough with
10 oz (M 280 gm, A 2½ C) 100% stoneground flour
15 oz (M 425 gm, A 3¾ C) rye flour
¾ oz (M 21 gm, A 1¼ cake) fresh yeast
1 dessert (M 1 dessert, A 1¼ dessert) salt
14½ oz (M 426 ml, A scant 1¾ C) warm water
1 dessert (M 1 dessert, A 1¼ dessert) molasses
1 table (M 1 table, A 1¼ table) carraway seeds, if liked

Add a little of the water to the yeast and leave for 10 minutes.
Make a well in the flour in the mixing bowl and add the yeast and the lump of risen sourdough and carraways.
Knead well and leave to rise inside a closed polythene bag for 2 hours. Rye flour always takes longer to rise.
Remove and shape into 3 small loaves.
Brush with milk
Prove for 30 to 40 minutes
Bake at 375°F (190°C, Gas Mark 5) for 40 minutes, or until hollow-sounding when tapped on the base.

White Breads and Rolls

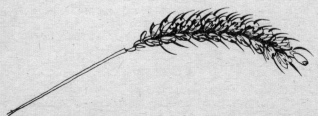

HASTY LOAF*

RECIPE CREATED BY THE AUTHOR

This loaf is a timesaver, but owing to the omission of the second rising, the texture is open and crumbly. It is best eaten fairly soon as there is no fat to keep it moist. An easy bread to make in emergencies.

1 Loaf

Ingredients

1 lb (M 450 gm, A 4 C) strong white flour

1 tsp (M 1 tsp, A 1¼ tsp) salt

½ oz (M 15 gm, A ¾ cake) fresh yeast

½ pint (M ¼ litre, A 1¼ C) warm milk and water, mixed

Method

1. Dissolve the yeast in a little of the warm liquid.
2. Add the salt to the flour and put in a large basin. Make a well in the centre and add the yeasty liquid.
3. Mix to a dough, adding remaining liquid and knead thoroughly for 10 minutes until the dough is silky and smooth.
4. Have ready a greased loaf tin and press the dough into the tin, especially into the corners to make sure of a good shape.
5. Rise inside a closed polythene bag until doubled in size.
6. Glaze with the top of the milk.
7. Put in a hot oven 425°F (220°C, Gas Mark 7) for 15 minutes. Reduce the heat after 15 minutes to 375°F (190°C, Gas Mark 5) and cook for a further 25 minutes. Cook for the last 5 minutes out of the tin to obtain a really crisp base crust.

SESAME SEED PLAIT*

This is a versatile recipe and the dough can be used in a variety of ways and shapes. It is a milk plait with a proportion of egg and fat and therefore keeps moist and also freezes well. Good with either homemade jam or savoury spreads.

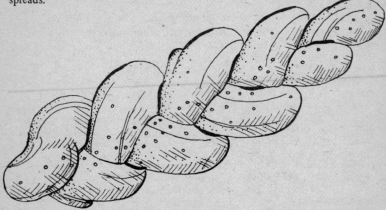

1 Plait

Ingredients

1 lb (M 450 gm, A 4 C) strong white flour

1 tsp (M 1 tsp, A 1¼ tsp) salt

½ oz (M 15 gm, A ¾ cake) dried yeast

1 tsp (M 1 tsp, A 1¼ tsp) white sugar

½ pint (M ¼ litre, A 1¼ C) warm milk

2 oz (M 55 gm, A ¼ C) margarine

1 beaten egg

Method

1. Cream yeast with the sugar and add half the milk.
2. Leave to froth up.
3. Put the flour in a bowl with the salt and make a well.
4. Melt the margarine, cool and add to the beaten egg.
5. Pour yeast and the rest of the liquids into the well.
6. Mix well and knead until smooth, adding extra flour if needed.
7. Rise inside a closed polythene bag until doubled. This takes about 1 hour.
8. Take out and shape into a plait.
9. Prove inside a closed polythene bag for 20 minutes.
10. Glaze with egg yolk and sprinkle thickly with sesame seeds.
11. Bake in a hot oven 425°F (220°C, Gas Mark 7) for 30 minutes, or until golden brown and cooked through.

BLENDER ROLLS*

These rolls are simply delicious; they freeze well, keep well, are easy and quick to prepare, and are a perfect all-purpose bread.

20 Rolls

Ingredients

8 fl oz (M 225 ml, A 1 C) warm water

1 table (M 1 table, A 1¼ table) dried yeast

1 tsp (M 1 tsp, A 1¼ tsp) white granulated sugar

¼ pint (M 140 ml, A ¾ cup) of cooking oil

1 egg

2 tsp (M 2 tsp, A 2½ tsp) salt

1 lb (M 450 gm, A 4 C) strong white flour

1 oz (M 30 gm, A 2 table) cooking fat

Poppy seeds to garnish

Method

1. Put the first 3 ingredients in the blender and leave for 5 minutes.
2. Blend for 15 seconds.
3. Add oil, egg and salt and blend for 5 seconds.
4. In the mixer bowl rub the fat into the flour, make a well in the centre and pour in the liquids.
5. Using a dough hook, knead for 3 minutes or until the dough is smooth and silky.
6. Place in a closed polythene bag and rise for 40-60 minutes.
7. Knock back, tip onto a floured board and divide into 20 pieces.
8. Roll under the hands into 6" (M 15cm) strands, knot loosely and place on a damp baking tin.
9. Prove inside a closed polythene bag for 20 minutes.
10. Brush over with top of the milk. Poppy seeds can be sprinkled generously over the batch. Bake at 400°F (200°C, Gas Mark 6) for 20 minutes.
11. A tin of boiling water in the base of the oven helps to make the crusts really crisp.

WHITE BREAD*

This is the basic white bread dough with a fair proportion of fat for keeping qualities. Dried fruit can be added to the dough to make a currant loaf. This dough is also suitable for a pizza base.

2 Large or 4 Small Loaves

Ingredients

2½ lb (M 1¼ kg, A 10 C) strong white flour

3 tsp (M 3 tsp, A 3¼ tsp) sea salt

1 oz (M 30 gm, A 1½ cake) fresh yeast

2 oz (M 55 gm, A ¼ C) margarine or butter—melted

1 pint (M ½ litre, A 2½ C) warm water

Method

Use the same method as for Wholemeal bread (see page 32). If the liquid is insufficient, add a little more, as flours vary in their absorbency.

Shape as desired, prove in a closed polythene bag until doubled in bulk, glaze with milk and bake at 400°F (200°C, Gas Mark 6) for 40 minutes.

ALITO ROLLS*

This recipe was given to me by the Mother Superior of a Mission Hospital in Northern Uganda. Her kitchen was small and dark but spotlessly clean. A minute iron Dover stove was the sole cooking aid. Mother Gabriella showed me how to make the rolls, while a small African boy stoked the stove with grass and wood. All her measurements were in either handfulls or glasses. I give you the abridged version of these very excellent crisp rolls. It is essential to have a dish of boiling water on the bottom of the oven to harden the crusts.

14 Rolls

Ingredients

9 oz (M 250 gm, A 1 heaped C) strong white flour

1 heaped dessert (M 1 heaped dessert, A 1 table) dried yeast

¼ pint (M 140 ml, A ¾ C) warmed milk

½ dessert (M ½ dessert, A 3 tsp) salt

1 mean dessert (M 1 mean dessert, A 1 table) white granulated sugar

4 dessert (M 4 dessert, A 3 table) corn oil

Method

1. Dissolve the yeast in the milk and sugar.
2. Put half the sugar and all of the salt in a bowl.
3. Make a well and add yeast.
4. Flick the flour over the well and leave for 30 minutes.
5. Add rest of flour and oil.
6. Mix and knead.
7. Rise inside a closed polythene bag for 1 hour or until doubled in size.
8. Knock back.
9. Leave 40 minutes.
10. Roll out into a long sausage on a floured board.
11. Cut into 14 pieces and roll under the hands.
12. Place on a floured baking sheet.
13. Prove in a closed polythene bag for 10 minutes.
14. Spray with salt water and bake at 425°F (220°C, Gas Mark 7) for 15-20 minutes.

Bacon Ring Loaf**

RECIPE CREATED BY THE AUTHOR

One of the nicest breads I've made! Delicious eaten warm with boiled eggs.

1 Large Ring

Ingredients

1½ lb (M 675 gm, A 6 C)
strong white flour

½ oz (M 15 gm, A ¾ cake)
fresh yeast

2 oz (M 55gm, A ¼ C)
margarine

1 tsp (M 1 tsp, A 1¼ tsp) salt

½ pint (M ¼ litre, A 1¼ C)
warm milk and water mixed

4 oz (M 115 gm, A 1 C) crisp
bacon pieces, crumbled small

Method

1. Cream the yeast with a little of the liquid and leave to froth.
2. Melt and cool the margarine.
3. Put flour and salt into a bowl.
4. Pour in the yeast liquid, mix and knead well.
5. Add the bacon pieces and continue to knead.
6. Rise inside a closed polythene bag for 40 minutes.
7. Grease a ring mould and press the dough down into the tin. The finished loaf cuts into small pieces.
8. Cut the top with scissors to form a pattern.
9. Prove until doubled in size.
10. Glaze with milk and bake at 400°F (200°C, Gas Mark 6) for 50 minutes or until dark brown and cooked through.

Baps**

Scotland's equivalent of our breakfast roll. The crust of a bap is traditionally floury and soft. Ideal to fill with frankfurters or hamburgers for a teenage barbecue.

6 Large Baps

Ingredients

1 lb (M 450 gm, A 4 C) strong
white flour
1 tsp (M 1 tsp, A 1¼ tsp) salt
2 oz (M 55 gm, A ¼ C) cooking fat
½ oz (M 15 gm, A ¾ cake) fresh yeast
½ pint (M ¼ litre, A 1¼ C) lukewarm
milk and water mixed

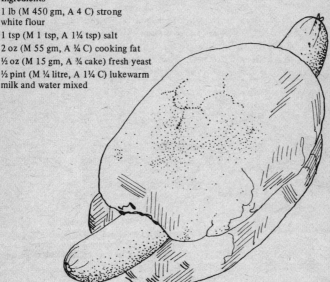

Method

1. Put the flour and salt in a bowl and make a well.
2. Rub in the fat.
3. Cream the yeast with a little liquid and leave to froth.
4. Pour all liquids into the well and mix.
5. Knead thoroughly.
6. Rise inside a closed polythene bag until doubled in bulk.
7. Knock back and re-knead lightly.
8. Divide dough into 6 equal sized pieces.
9. Shape each under the hand into round balls and roll with a pin to flatten the top.
10. Place well apart on floured baking sheets and prick all over with a skewer.
11. Dredge with flour and prove in a closed polythene bag until doubled.
12. Bake at 400°F (200°C, Gas Mark 6) for 20 minutes.

Note: A wheatmeal bap can be made using this recipe by substituting half the strong white flour for farmhouse 81% flour and adding extra liquid because this flour is more absorbent.

Black Olive Plait**

RECIPE CREATED BY THE AUTHOR

While on a visit to Turkey, I tasted some unleavened bread spread with chopped unripe olives. The flavour was memorable, but it was rather heavy, solid textured bread, and so I decided to try and prepare a bread of a lighter quality. It eats well with all meats and savouries, especially cream cheese. The dough can be shaped into all types of loaves and rolls.

1 Plait

Ingredients

1¼ lb (M 565 gm, A 4½ C) strong white flour

½ oz (M 15 gm, A ¾ cake) fresh yeast

1 oz (M 30 gm, A 2 table) butter, margarine, or lard

2 tsp (M 2 tsp, A 2½ tsp) salt

1 dozen stoned black olives, chopped

1 pint (M ½ litre, A 2½ C) warm water

Method

1. Cream the yeast with a little of the liquid.
2. Melt the fat.
3. Put flour and salt into a bowl.
4. Make a well in the centre and pour in the fat, yeast and warm water.
5. Mix well and knead until smooth.
6. Add extra liquid, if needed.
7. Rise inside a closed polythene bag for 1½ - 2 hours, or until doubled in size.
8. Knock back and roll out into an oblong on a floured board. Sprinkle with chopped olives overall. Roll up tightly. Roll out again and plait*.
9. Glaze with beaten egg yolk.
10. Bake at 400°F (200°C, Gas Mark 6) for 40 minutes, or longer for a dark brown crisp crust.

*See 'Shapes' on page 18.

Cheese Plait**

In this recipe the dough is slow to rise because the cheese retards the action of the yeast. The finished loaf is close textured and is at its best eaten fresh with cream cheese and salad. Sandwiches of cucumber and tomato and a sprinkling of fresh parsley taste delicious.

2 Plaits

Ingredients

1½ lb (M 675 gm, A 6 C) strong white flour

3 tsp (M 3 tsp, A 3¾ tsp) sea salt

1 tsp (M 1 tsp, A 1¼ tsp) white granulated sugar

1 oz (M 30 gm, A 1½ cake) fresh yeast

1 tsp (M 1 tsp, A 1¼ tsp) black pepper

2 dessert (M 2 dessert, A 1 table) wheat germ

6 oz (M 170 gm, A 1½ C) grated sharp dry cheese, e.g. Lancashire

¾ pint (M 425 ml, A 2 C) warm water

Method

1. Cream yeast and sugar with a little of the warm water.
2. Put dry ingredients in a bowl.
3. Make a well in the centre.
4. Pour in yeast liquid and mix.
5. Add remainder of water and mix. It will make a rather slack mixture. Flour hands to knead.
6. Rise inside a closed polythene bag for 1 hour.
7. Sprinkle board thickly with flour, turn dough out on to it, and knock back. Shape into two plaits*.
8. Prove inside a closed polythene bag for 20 minutes.
9. Glaze with eggwash and bake at 400°F (200°C, Gas Mark 6) for 30-40 minutes.

*See 'Shapes' on page 18.

Cornmeal ** Sesame Batons

RECIPE CREATED BY THE AUTHOR

This is a fatless loaf and should be eaten soon after baking. It is best with strong cheese and olives. If a crisper crust is preferred, spray the loaves with water every 15 minutes during the baking.

2 Batons

Ingredients

1½ lb (M 675 gm, A 6 C) strong white flour

2 oz (M 55 gm, A ½ C) cornmeal or polenta

2 table (M 2 table, A 2½ table) salt

1 table (M 1 table, A 1¼ table) white granulated sugar

3 table (M 3 table, A 3¾ table) sesame seeds

2 oz (M 55 gm, A 3 cake) fresh yeast

1 pint (M ½ litre, A 2½ C) warm water

Method

1. Dissolve the yeast in half the water with the sugar.
2. Add cornmeal to flour and place in a large bowl.
3. Add the yeast liquid.
4. Mix and add more water until a pliable dough is obtained.
5. Knead well.
6. Place in a closed polythene bag to rise for 40 minutes.
7. Divide into three and roll each piece into a thin sausage.
8. Place on greased and floured sheets.
9. Put into a cold oven on the lowest shelf. The bread will rise in the oven.
10. Turn the oven to 350°F (180°C, Gas Mark 4) and bake for 1½ hours or until golden brown.

French Baton**

The main attraction of the French baton lies in the crust. The commercial steam ovens can produce this crust, but the housewife can produce as crisp a crust with the aid of a tin of boiling water in the base of the oven, and by frequently spraying the baking loaves with water. The flour which produces the true French loaf is also different, and is not easily obtainable outside France. I find that this loaf is delicious eaten fresh with plenty of unsalted butter and some good French garlic cheese!

1 Large or 2 Small Batons

Ingredients

1 lb (M 450 gm, A 4 C) strong white flour

¼ tsp (M ¼ tsp, A ¼ tsp) salt

½ oz (M 15 gm, A ¾ cake) fresh yeast

½ pint (M ¼ litre, A 1¼ C) warm water

1 oz (M 30 gm, A 2 table) margarine or butter—melted

¼ tsp (M ¼ tsp, A ¼ tsp) granulated sugar

Method

1. Cream yeast and sugar and add water.
2. Stir in the flour and salt and melted butter. Knead well. The dough is putty-like.
3. Leave to rise inside a closed polythene bag at room temperature.
4. Knock back and leave again until doubled in bulk.
5. Roll out into an oblong shape and roll up very tightly by hand as a baton.
6. Place on a greased baking tin and slash three times with a sharp knife.
7. Prove for 30 minutes inside a polythene bag.
8. Spray with cold water and bake at 425°F (220°C, Gas Mark 7) for 15 minutes.
9. Spray again with water to develop a crisp strong crust. Bake a further 15-20 minutes at 400°F (200°C, Gas Mark 6).

Onion Bread**

This is another type of dough which can be formed into either loaves or rolls. Onion bread keeps and freezes well. It is at its best eaten with cream cheese or ham salad.

2 Loaves

Ingredients

3 oz (M 85 gm, A ¾ C) dried onions soaked in
¼ pint (M 140 ml, A ¾ C) warm water
1 lb 2 oz (M 500 gm, A 4¼ C) strong
white bread flour
2 tsp (M 2 tsp, A 2½ tsp) salt
1 oz (M 30 gm, A 1½ cake) fresh yeast
1 tsp (M 1 tsp, A 1¼ tsp) white sugar
12 screws of black pepper
1 tsp (M 1 tsp, A 1¼ tsp) prepared mustard
8 oz (M 220 ml, A 1 C) warm water

Method

1. Soak the dried onions for 5 minutes in the warm water.
2. Strain. Cream the yeast in the onion water with the sugar.
3. Put the flour, onions, salt, mustard and pepper in a bowl.
4. Make a well, add yeast and slowly work in remainder of water.
5. Mix well and knead with floured hands as this is a soft dough.
6. Rise for 1 hour or until doubled, inside a closed polythene bag.
7. Shape into 2 oblongs.
8. Roll up Swiss roll fashion, and press into 2 greased tins.
9. Prove inside a closed polythene bag for 20 minutes.
10. Glaze the loaves with beaten egg and sprinkle the tops with coarse salt.
11. Bake at 400°F (200°C, Gas Mark 6) for 20 minutes and at 350°F (180°C, Gas Mark 4) for a further 30 minutes until golden brown and cooked through.

PLAITED MILK BREAD**

This recipe uses a dough enriched with milk and egg. The dough can be shaped into plaits, rolls or, with a generous handful of dried fruit added, into a delicious tea bread with a plain water icing topping. Milk bread is ideal for toasting and for sandwiches.

2 Plaits

Ingredients

1 lb (M 450 gm, A 4 C) strong white flour

1 heaped tsp (M 1 heaped tsp, A 1¼ tsp) salt

½ oz (M 15 gm, A ¾ cake) fresh yeast

1 tsp (M 1 tsp, A 1¼ tsp) white sugar

½ pint (M ¼ litre, A 1¼ C) warm milk

2 oz (M 55 gm, A ¼ C) margarine

1 egg

Poppy seeds and glaze

Method

1. Cream sugar and yeast
2. Add a little milk and leave until frothy.
3. Mix salt with flour and rub in fat.
4. Add yeast liquid and beaten egg.
5. Mix well and knead to an elastic dough.
6. Place in a closed polythene bag and rise until doubled.
7. Knock back on a floured board. Divide into two.
8. Plait each piece* and place on a greased tin in a closed polythene bag to prove for 20 minutes.
9. Glaze with beaten egg or milk and sprinkle with poppy seeds.
10. Bake at 400°F (200°C, Gas Mark 6) for 30-40 minutes.

*See 'Shapes' on page 18

Salted Bread Sticks **

Very good indeed with hot soups of all kinds!

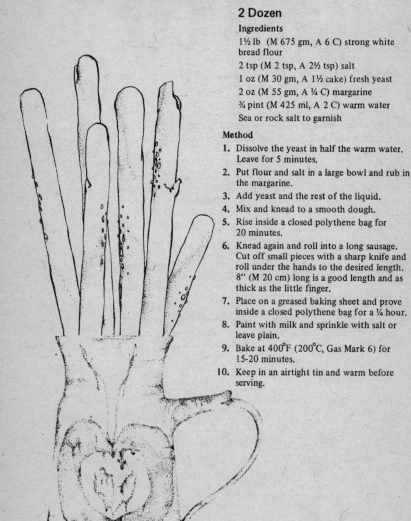

2 Dozen

Ingredients

1½ lb (M 675 gm, A 6 C) strong white bread flour

2 tsp (M 2 tsp, A 2½ tsp) salt

1 oz (M 30 gm, A 1½ cake) fresh yeast

2 oz (M 55 gm, A ¼ C) margarine

¾ pint (M 425 ml, A 2 C) warm water

Sea or rock salt to garnish

Method

1. Dissolve the yeast in half the warm water. Leave for 5 minutes.
2. Put flour and salt in a large bowl and rub in the margarine.
3. Add yeast and the rest of the liquid.
4. Mix and knead to a smooth dough.
5. Rise inside a closed polythene bag for 20 minutes.
6. Knead again and roll into a long sausage. Cut off small pieces with a sharp knife and roll under the hands to the desired length. 8″ (M 20 cm) long is a good length and as thick as the little finger.
7. Place on a greased baking sheet and prove inside a closed polythene bag for a ¼ hour.
8. Paint with milk and sprinkle with salt or leave plain.
9. Bake at 400°F (200°C, Gas Mark 6) for 15-20 minutes.
10. Keep in an airtight tin and warm before serving.

TOMATO
BREAD**

Tomato bread is as attractive to look at as it is to eat. If baked in a small loaf tin, then made into sandwiches with a green filling of either cucumber or watercress, it looks very decorative. It is a good accompaniment to all savoury meals.

1 Plait or 20 Rolls

Ingredients

½ pint (M ¼ litre, A 1¼ C) warm water

1 tsp (M 1 tsp, A 1¼ tsp) strong white flour

1 level table (M 1 table, A 1¼ table) dried yeast

1½ lb (M 675 gm, A 6 C) strong white flour

2 tsp (M 2 tsp, A 2½ tsp) salt

2 tsp (M 2 tsp, A 2½ tsp) paprika

¼ pint (M 140 ml, A ¾ C) tomato juice

3 table (M 3 table, A 3¾ table) cooking oil

Poppy seeds to garnish

Method

1. Place the first 4 items in the blender.
2. Leave to stand for 5 minutes to allow the yeast to work.
3. Blend for 15 seconds.
4. Place the remaining ingredients in the mixer bowl, except the poppy seeds.
5. Make a well in the flour, fit the dough hook and knead for 3 minutes. Add extra flour until the dough leaves the sides of the bowl. The dough is a very slack one.
6. Rise inside an oiled polythene bag for 1 hour or until doubled. Proving time and rising time all depend on the surrounding temperature.*
7. Turn onto a floured board and shape into rolls, cobs or a plait.†
8. Prove for 20 minutes inside a closed polythene bag, glaze with milk and scatter poppy seeds over the top. Bake at 400°F (200°C, Gas Mark 6). Rolls will take 20 minutes and loaves up to 40 minutes.

*See the section on Rising on page 22
†See 'Shapes' on page 18

BRIOCHE***

A classic French breakfast bread, the brioche is rich in eggs and butter, which give a cake-like texture with a feathery crust. In France, the brioche is used in a variety of ways, both sweet and savoury. Cake flour can be used instead of the strong white flour, with equally good results.

16 Brioche

Ingredients

8 oz (M 225 gm, A 2 C) strong white flour

5 oz (M 145 gm, A 1 heaped C) strong white flour

3 eggs

½ oz (M 15 gm, A ¾ cake) fresh yeast, dissolved in

1 dessert (M 1 dessert, A 1¼ dessert) warm water

½ tsp (M ½ tsp, A ¾ tsp) salt

4 oz (M 115 gm, A ½ C) unsalted butter

1 oz (M 30 gm, A 2 table) sugar

4 fl oz (M 110 ml, A ½ C) warm milk

Method

1. Beat the eggs and the warm milk in a large bowl.

2. Cream the yeast and water and add to the eggs and milk.

3. Melt the butter and add to the eggs and milk.

4. Whisk together with a loop whisk, adding the first measure of flour gradually.

5. Leave for 1 hour inside a closed polythene bag.

6. Beat hard with a wooden spoon and add the second measure of flour gradually. The dough will be a slack one and it will be easier to work with a spoon rather than the hand. An electric mixer and dough hook are a great advantage here. Don't be tempted to add too much flour or the finished brioche will be tough.

7. Cover the bowl with plastic wrapping and leave overnight in the refrigerator.

8. Next day, knock back and tip out onto a well floured board. Flour your hands too. Divide dough into 16 pieces. Have ready oiled brioche tins or castle pudding tins.

9. Shape the pieces of dough into oblongs and drop into the prepared tins. Snip off a small portion of the dough with a pair of kitchen scissors for the 'head' of the brioche.

10. Make a hole in the top of the brioche with the handle of a spoon and refit the snipped off pieces of dough.

11. Prove inside a closed polythene bag for 30 minutes.

12. Glaze with egg yolk and bake at 425°F (220°C, Gas Mark 7) for 30-35 minutes.

Croissants***

These unique French breakfast rolls should always be eaten hot.
Feather-light and delicate, they have a delectable buttery flavour.

18 Small Croissants

Ingredients

10 oz (M 280 gm, A 2½ C) strong
bread flour
1 tsp (M 1 tsp, A 1¼ tsp) salt
1 table (M 1 table, A 1¼ table) melted
unsalted butter
1 table (M 1 table, A 1¼ table) white
granulated sugar

½ oz (M 15 gm, A 3 tsp) dried yeast
¼ pint (M 140 ml, A ¾ C) warm milk
4 oz (M 110 gm, A ½ C) unsalted butter—
well chilled

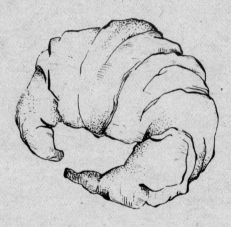

Method

1. Soak the yeast in a little warm milk and
   the sugar and leave for 5 minutes.
2. Add melted but cooled butter.
3. Put the flour and salt in a bowl and
   make a well.
4. Pour in the liquids.
5. Mix well and knead until smooth.
6. Rise inside a closed polythene bag for
   1 hour.

7. Take out and have ready a floured board.

8. Roll out the dough into a long strip, as for puff pastry.

9. Spread the chilled butter in flakes over 2/3 of the dough, leaving the bottom 1/3 uncovered. Don't put the butter near the edges as it will ooze out with successive rollings. Leave 1" (M 2½ cm) on either side.

10. Bring the top third down to the centre and the bottom third up and over, forming a parcel. Roll with the rolling pin to seal ends.

11. Give a half turn and repeat rolling and folding twice more.

12. Wrap in plastic film and chill for 30 minutes in the coldest part of the refrigerator, next to the ice compartment.

13. Take out, roll and fold three times.

14. Chill for another 30 minutes in a polythene bag, then take out and roll twice. Leave for 7 hours or overnight well wrapped in plastic film. The dough will rise slowly all the time.

15. Take out and roll into a ¼" (M 6mm) thick square. Measure off 4" (M 10 cm) squares with a ruler (or make a cardboard template).

16. Cut each square in half into triangles.

17. Roll up from the long side to the point. Seal the point with a dab of water and shape into crescents. The importance of even and careful shaping cannot be too strongly stressed, otherwise the finished croissants will be shapeless and will lose a lot of their attraction.

18. Place on a lightly floured tin, paint gently with beaten egg yolk and cream.

19. Have the oven ready heated to 425°F (220°C, Gas Mark 7). Bake at once without proving. Cooking time 20 minutes.

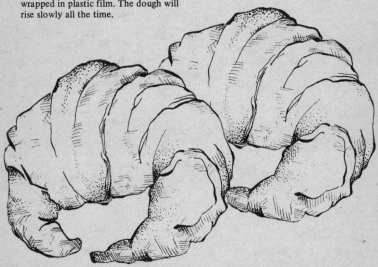

Note: I have found that the "no proving" method is more successful and produces shapely croissants in 20 minutes. The dough can be ready to draw on in the refrigerator and the croissants ready for breakfast any day of the week, once you have made a batch of dough. Keep it in a plastic box for up to a week. These croissants freeze well in polythene bags.

Oatmeal and Potato Bread***

RECIPE CREATED BY THE AUTHOR

The potato is a valuable addition to breadmaking in many countries. In parts of Africa, potato water is used as a yeast starter. This recipe produces a light textured moist loaf. Shaping can be done either in a tin or without. Small loaves baked without tins will be ready sooner. This is an all-purpose bread, but is particularly delicious with meat pâtés and red wine.

1 Plait and 1 Round Cob

Ingredients

1 large potato cut up and cooked in enough water to cover

¼ pint (M 140 ml, A ¾ C) warm potato water

10 fl oz (M 280 ml, A 1¼ C) skim milk

1½ tsp (M 1½ tsp, A 1¾ tsp) dried yeast

1 tsp (M 1 tsp, A 1¼ tsp) white granulated sugar

1½ table (M 1½ table, A 2 table) corn oil

1½ lb (M 675 gm, A 6 C) strong white flour

1 table (M 1 table, A 2 table) salt

8 oz (M 225 gm, A 2 C) porridge oats

Method

1. Dissolve the yeast in ¼ pint (M 140 ml, A ¾ C) warm potato water with the sugar.
2. Mash the potato with a little of the skim milk.
3. Mix remainder of the milk with the corn oil.
4. Pour flour and salt into a bowl. Make a well.
5. Add the liquids, the well-creamed potato and, lastly, the porridge oats.
6. Mix well and knead until silky smooth. The dough is a slack one.
7. Put to rise for 2 hours inside a closed polythene bag.
8. Knock back.
9. Rise for a further 30 minutes. Divide into three pieces. On a floured board, roll out two pieces into long, rounded strips and plait together. Shape the third into a cob.* Prove both loaves inside a polythene bag until doubled in size.
10. Glaze with beaten egg and sprinkle with oats.
11. Bake at 425°F (220°C, Gas Mark 7) for 40 minutes. Loaves baked without tins will take up to 30 minutes.

*See 'Shapes' on pages 18 and 19

Tea Breads and Buns

Overnight Tea Bread*

Here is a tea bread which uses tea as an ingredient, giving an added piquancy to this sweet and spicy loaf. A simple recipe—and the finished loaf keeps moist for several days and also freezes well. To be eaten sliced and buttered.

2 Small Loaves

Ingredients

1 lb (M 450 gm, A 4 C) self-raising 81% flour

A good pinch of salt added

1 tsp (M 1 tsp, A 1¼ tsp) ground cinnamon

1 tsp (M 1tsp, A 1¼ tsp) mixed spice

1 lb (M 450 gm, A 3 C) mixed dried fruit

8 oz (M 225 gm, A 1 C) dark brown soft sugar

4 oz (M 115 gm, A 2/3 C) chopped dates

8 fl oz (M 225 ml, A 1 C) hot tea, freshly made

2 large eggs, beaten

2 table (M 2 table, A 2½ table) lime marmalade

Method

1. Put fruit, sugar and tea in a bowl and leave overnight.
2. Next day add the rest of the ingredients.
3. Mix thoroughly and divide between two small foil lined bread tins.
4. Bake at 325°F (170°C, Gas Mark 3) for 1-1½ hours.

Treacle and Raisin Bread*

The combination of the wholemeal flour and treacle makes this loaf dark and very delicious. Try and obtain the large sticky seedless raisins from a health food shop, as they have so much more flavour than the ordinary packeted variety. Honey can replace the treacle for a change. Slice and butter for tea.

2 Small Loaves

Ingredients

1 lb (M 450 gm, A 3½ C) wholemeal flour

2 oz (M 55 gm, A ¼ C) margarine

1 tsp (M 1 tsp, A 1¼ tsp) salt

½ oz (M 15 gm, A ¾ cake) fresh yeast

1 tsp (M 1 tsp, A 1¼ tsp) caster sugar

2 table (M 2 table, A 2½ table) black treacle

½ pint (M ¼ litre, A 1¼ C) boiling water

4 oz (M 115 gm, A 2/3 C) stoned chopped raisins

2 oz (M 55 gm, A 1/3 C) currants

Method

1. Put the treacle in a bowl and add the boiling water. Leave until lukewarm.

2. Cream the yeast with the sugar.

3. Put the flour in a bowl and rub in the margarine. Add the salt.

4. Make a well and pour in the yeast and treacle water.

5. Mix well and add the dried fruit.

6. Knead or use 'K' beater on the electric mixer, as the dough is slack.

7. Rise inside a closed polythene bag until doubled in bulk—approximately 1 hour.

8. Shape lightly on a floured board into 2 loaves.

9. Press into greased tins and prove inside a polythene bag for 20-30 minutes.

10. Brush over with milk and bake at 425°F (220°C, Gas Mark 7) for one hour or until dry when skewer tested.

Walnut and Raisin Tea Bread*

A simple recipe for another appetizing fruit and nut flavoured tea bread. To be sliced thick and buttered.

1 Loaf

Ingredients

1¼ lb (M 565 gm, A 4½ C) soft white flour

2 tsp (M 2 tsp, A 2½ tsp) baking powder

2 eggs, beaten

6 oz (M 170 gm, A 1½ C) soft brown sugar

5 oz (M 145 gm, A ½ C + 2 table) lard

4 oz (M 115 gm, A 2/3 C) stoned raisins, chopped

2 oz (M 55 gm, A 1/3 C) walnuts, chopped

Cold milk to mix

Method

1. Rub lard into the flour.
2. Add baking powder.
3. Add sugar, fruit and nuts.
4. Beat the eggs and add sufficient milk to give a fairly stiff mixture.
5. Press into a greased square meat tin lined with foil.
6. Bake at 325°F (170°C, Gas Mark 3) for 1 hour. Leave in tin until the following day.

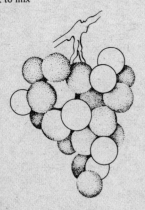

Banana Tea Loaf**

A delicious, rich, delicately flavoured tea bread. Best if kept wrapped in foil for a day before slicing and buttering thickly for tea.

1 Loaf

Ingredients

8 oz (M 225 gm, A 1¾ C) 81% self-raising flour
½ tsp (M ½ tsp, A ¾ tsp) salt
¼ tsp (M ¼ tsp, A ¼ tsp) bicarbonate of soda
2 oz (M 55 gm, A ¼ C) margarine or butter
1 table (M 1 table, A 1¼ table) corn oil
4 oz (M 115 gm, A ½ C) soft brown sugar
2 beaten eggs
1 lb (M 450 gm) or 3 - 4 medium size ripe mashed bananas

Method

1. Cream butter and sugar.
2. Add eggs and beat well.
3. Mash bananas and add.
4. Fold in flour, soda and salt and put mixture into a greased 1 lb (M 450 gm) bread tin.
5. Bake at 350°F (180°C Gas Mark 4) for 1 hour and 15 minutes.

Cardamom Plait*

An exotic, spicy tea bread, easy to make. A particular favourite with my family. Serve warm with unsalted butter.

1 Large Plait

Ingredients

1½ lb (M 675 gm, A 6 C) strong white flour

¼ tsp (M ¼ tsp, A ¼ heaped tsp) ground cardamom

½ pint (M ¼ litre, A 1¼ C) warmed milk

4 oz (M 115 gm, A ½ C) melted butter

1 egg—beaten

4 oz (M 115 gm, A ½ C) caster sugar

Beaten egg to glaze

Method

1. Cream the yeast with a little of the sugar and milk.

2. Beat the egg and add to the remainder of the milk.

3. Put the flour and cardamom with sugar into a bowl.

4. Make a well in the centre and pour in all the liquids. Mix well.

5. Knead until smooth and rise inside a closed polythene bag for 1 hour, or until doubled in size.

6. Knock back and shape into a plait*.

7. Prove on a floured baking tray in a closed polythene bag for 30 minutes.

8. Bake at 425°F (220°C, Gas Mark 7) for 30 minutes.

9. Brush with glaze after the plait has been in the oven for 5 minutes.

Note: I have given the minimum quantity of cardamom here. Anything up to 2 teaspoons can be used. Coriander is also very nice, not being as strong as cardamom.

*See 'Shapes' on page 18

FATLESS NUT TEA BREAD*

An unusual tea bread with a pleasant fruit and nut flavour. In this recipe some of the ingredients can be substituted to make a change. The golden syrup could be exchanged for an equal quantity of molasses or treacle. The dried fruit could be a mixture of fruits or another fruit, e.g. figs or dates. It should be wrapped in foil and kept in a tin for a day before slicing and buttering for tea.

1 Loaf

Ingredients

12 oz (M 340 gm, A 3 C) self-raising flour

4 oz (M 115 gm, A ½ C) soft brown sugar

4 oz (M 115 gm, A 2/3 C) dried apricots, cut up or minced

4 oz (M 115 gm, A ½ C) walnuts—crushed or minced

4 oz (M 115 gm, A 2/3 C) sultanas or raisins

4 level table (M 4 level table, A ¼ C) syrup—melted but cool

2 large eggs, beaten with:

6 table (M 6 table, A ¼ C) milk

Method

1. Put all the dry ingredients into a bowl.
2. Make a well and add the rest of the ingredients.
3. Mix carefully.
4. Spoon into a greased 2 lb (M 1 kg) loaf tin.
5. Bake at 325°F (170°C, Gas Mark 3) for 1½-2 hours.

CORNISH SPLITS**

These gorgeous little squashy buns are definitely worth getting fat for!
The traditional cream and strawberry jam accompaniment is a 'must'.
Equally good with a savoury filling for picnics. They freeze well and only
need to be rewarmed for immediate eating.

24 Splits

Ingredients

1 lb (M 450 gm, A 4 C) strong
white flour

1 tsp (M 1 tsp, A 1¼ tsp) salt

¾ oz (M 20 gm, A 1¼ cake) fresh yeast

1 tsp (M 1 tsp, A 1¼ tsp) granulated sugar

1 oz (M 30 gm, A 2 table) butter

½ pint (M ¼ litre, A 1¼ C) warm skim
milk *or* ½ pint (M ¼ litre, A 1¼ C) water
+ 2 table (M 2 table, A 2½ table) skim
milk powder

Method

1. Melt the butter and cool.
2. Cream the yeast and sugar together
   with half the milk and leave for
   5 minutes to froth up.
3. Put the flour in a bowl and make
   a well.
4. Pour in the melted butter and
   yeast mixture.
5. Mix and knead well. The dough is
   a soft one.
6. Rise for 1 hour and 10 minutes in
   a closed polythene bag.
7. Turn out onto a well floured board
   and knead until the dough is soft
   and elastic.
8. With a floured rolling pin, roll out
   like pastry and cut with a scone
   cutter ¾" (M 2cm) thick. The size
   is a matter of taste. I think the
   smaller the better.
9. Put on a floured baking sheet fairly
   close together so that in rising they
   support each other.
10. Prove in a closed polythene bag
    for 10 minutes.
11. Paint with top of the milk and bake
    in a hot oven 425°F (220°C, Gas
    Mark 7) for 10-15 minutes.

Strawberry
Jam

QUINCE TEA BREAD**

This is a delicious, unusual loaf which keeps and freezes well. In England, quinces are in season in October, and the purée can be the contents of the jelly bag put through a mouli. The flavour is enhanced if the bread is cut, buttered, and spread with a thin layer of quince jelly.

2 Small Loaves

Ingredients

8 oz (M 225 gm, A 1¾ C) wholemeal self-raising flour

7 oz (M 200 gm, A 1¾ C) strong white flour

½ tsp (M ½ tsp, A ¾ tsp) salt

1 tsp (M 1 tsp, A 1¼ tsp) bicarbonate of soda

1 tsp (M 1 tsp, A 1¼ tsp) baking powder

2 oz (M 55 gm, A ¼ C) butter

3 oz (M 85 gm, A 1/3 C) soft brown sugar

1 large egg

6 fl oz (M 170 ml, A ¾ C) unsweetened quince purée

8 fl oz (M 225 ml, A 1 C) yoghourt

6 oz (M 170 gm, A 1 C) broken walnuts

Method

1. Cream the fat and sugar until fluffy.
2. Add beaten egg, quince purée and nuts.
3. Mix the flours carefully with the soda and baking powder.
4. Add to the creamed mixture alternately with the yoghourt.
5. Stir with a metal spoon—*do not* beat the mixture.
6. Spoon the mixture into 2 well greased small loaf tins.
7. Bake at 350°F (180°C, Gas Mark 4) for 40-60 minutes

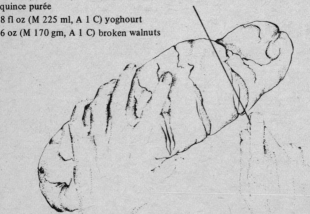

RECIPE CREATED BY THE AUTHOR

apple tea bread**

RECIPE CREATED BY THE AUTHOR

2 Small Loaves

Make as for Quince Tea Bread substituting the apple purée for quince purée. This bread is equally delicious and makes a change from the more usual tea-time treats!

CHELSEA BUNS*:

This bun needs no introduction! It is one of the best known English tea buns and very popular with children. Nicest when eaten warm the day they are made.

12 Buns

Ingredients

¾ lb (M 345 gm, A 3 C) strong white flour *and* a good pinch of salt

4 oz (M 115 gm, A ½ C) butter

½ oz (M 15 gm, A ¾ cake) fresh yeast

4 oz (M 115 gm, A ½ C) caster sugar

2 eggs

3 fl oz (M 90 ml, A ¾ C) warm milk

3 oz (M 85 gm, A 1/3 C) currants and mixed peel

Grated rind of 1 lemon

Sugar syrup to glaze*

*See 'Toppings' on page 26

Method

1. Cream the yeast with 1 tsp (M 1 tsp, A 1¼ tsp) sugar.
2. Add the warm milk.
3. Put the flour and salt in a bowl and make a well.
4. Rub in half the butter and half the sugar, add the rind.
5. Beat the eggs and add to the yeast liquid.
6. Pour all into the well. Mix and knead thoroughly.
7. Rise for 1 - 1½ hours inside a closed polythene bag. The rich mixture will rise by 1/3 only.
8. Roll out with a rolling pin on a floured board. With a spatula spread the remaining softened butter over the dough.
9. Sprinkle the remaining sugar and fruit over. With floured hands, roll up tightly like a Swiss roll.
10. Cut in 1½″ (4cm) slices with a very sharp knife.
11. Place the buns close together on a floured tin so that they rise and support each other.
12. Prove for 15 minutes inside a closed polythene bag.
13. Bake at 400°F (200°C, Gas Mark 6) for 20 minutes or until light golden.
14. Take out and brush over with sugar syrup.
15. Return to the oven for 3 minutes and then cool on a rack.

CURRANT BUNS**

Always a tea-time favourite, the currant bun is good with butter and honey. Especially tempting when warmed first, or toasted. The same recipe can be used to make a tea time currant loaf.

12 Buns

Ingredients

¾ lb (M 345 gm, A 3 C) strong white flour
½ oz (M 15 gm, A ¾ cake) fresh yeast
2 oz (M 55 gm, A ¼ C) margarine
2 oz (M 55 gm, A ¼ C) caster sugar
¼ pint (M 140 ml, A ¾ C) warmed skim milk
2 oz (M 55 gm, A ¼ C) currants
Liquid honey to glaze

Method

1. Cream the yeast with a little warm milk and 1 tsp (M 1 tsp, A 1¼ tsp) caster sugar.
2. Put the flour in a bowl and add the salt and remaining sugar.
3. Melt the margarine and add to the milk.
4. Pour liquids into the flour and mix well.
5. Add the currants.
6. Knead well and rise in a closed polythene bag for 1 hour or until doubled in size.
7. Knock back.
8. Take pieces the size of a ping-pong ball and roll under the hand.
9. Place on a floured sheet close together, so that the rising buns support one another.
10. Prove in a closed polythene bag until doubled in size.
11. Bake in a hot oven at 375°F (190°C, Gas Mark 5) for 30 minutes.
12. Remove from the oven and brush over with the liquid honey glaze. If a sweeter bun is desired, demerara sugar can be sprinkled on top before glazing.
13. Return to the oven for 5 minutes.

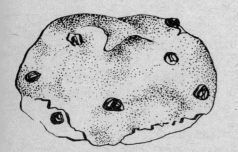

BATH BUNS**

Probably everyone is familiar with this traditional English tea bun. It has a rich, appetizing, fruity taste and can be eaten toasted with butter. Ideal for winter fireside teas!

16 Buns

Ingredients

1 lb (M 450 gm, A 4 C) strong white flour

1 table (M 1 table, A 1¼ table) caster sugar

1 oz (M 30 gm, A 1½ cake) fresh yeast

1 tsp (M 1 tsp, A 1¼ tsp) salt

6 fl oz (168 ml, A ¾ C) warm milk

8 oz (M 225 gm, A 1½ C) mixed fruit

2 oz (M 55 gm, A ¼ C) butter, melted and cooled

1 egg beaten

Milk, beaten egg and sugar crystals to finish

Method

1. Put the flour, salt, sugar and fruit into a bowl.
2. Cream the yeast with a little warm milk and leave for 5 minutes.
3. Beat the egg and add to the remaining milk
4. Pour all the liquids into the flour.
5. Mix thoroughly and knead well.
6. Add a little extra flour, if needed, to remove stickiness.
7. Rise inside a closed polythene bag until doubled in bulk.
8. Take tablespoons of dough and place on a buttered and floured baking sheet.
9. Prove inside a closed polythene bag for 25 minutes.
10. Brush over with beaten egg and milk to glaze, sprinkle with sugar crystals. Coloured coffee sugar or crushed cube sugar make good toppings.
11. Bake at 400°F (200°C, Gas Mark 6) for 20 minutes. If the buns are to be frozen, bake for 15 minutes only, to lessen the tendency to dryness when reheating.

Malt Loaf **

A dark, rich-tasting tea bread which should be cut thickly and buttered.
Keep wrapped in foil for a day before eating.

2 Loaves

Ingredients

1 lb 4 oz (M 565 gm, A 4½ C)
plain white flour

A good pinch of salt

1 tsp (M 1 tsp, A 1¼ tsp)
granulated sugar

½ oz (M 15 gm, A ¾ cake)
dried yeast

2 table (M 2 table, A 2½ table)
molasses

2 table (M 3 table, A 3¾ table)
malt extract

4 oz (M 115 gm, A 2/3 C) sultanas

1 oz (M 30 gm, A 2 table) lard

6 fl oz (M 170 ml, A ¾ C) warm
water

Method

1. Put the flour and salt into a bowl.
2. Melt fat, molasses and malt and cool.
3. Dissolve the yeast in a little water and sugar.
4. Pour everything into the flour and mix well.
5. If the mixture is too soft, add more flour.
6. Turn out onto floured working surface or pastry board and knead well.
7. Divide into two and punch each piece of dough into a small loaf tin.
8. Rise inside a closed polythene bag until the dough has doubled in size.
9. Glaze with milk and bake at 400°F (200°C, Gas Mark 6) for 40 minutes.

Note: For those people who prefer not to use white flour in baking, an 81% brown flour is satisfactory in this malt loaf. If all malt is used and the molasses omitted, the loaf will be much lighter in colour.

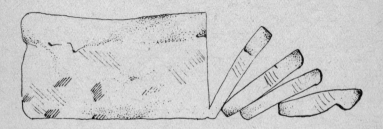

ORANGE TEA BREAD**

This is a delicious bread with a strong orange flavour. Very good when eaten with unsalted butter, or made into special-occasion sandwiches with cream cheese and chopped walnuts.

2 Loaves

Ingredients

1 lb (M 450 gm, A 4 C) strong white flour

1 whole, unpeeled orange, minced or liquidized

¼ pint (M 140 ml, A ¾ C) warm water and 5 table (M 5 table, A 6 table) diluted orange squash

1 oz (M 30 gm, A 1½ cake) dried yeast

1 tsp (M 1 tsp, A 1¼ tsp) salt

1 tsp (M 1 tsp, A 1¼ tsp) soft brown sugar

1 table (M 1 table, A 1¼ table) cooking oil

Honey glaze

Method

1. Mince or liquidize the orange and set aside.
2. Dissolve the yeast with the sugar and water.
3. Leave for 5 minutes.
4. Put the flour and salt in a bowl and make a well.
5. Pour in the yeast and orange.
6. Mix well.
7. Knead until smooth adding a little extra orange juice if necessary (bottled will do), and rise inside a closed polythene bag until doubled in size.
8. Knock back. Shape into two loaf tins.
9. Prove inside a closed polythene bag for 20 minutes.
10. Bake for 30 - 40 minutes at 400°F (200°C, Gas Mark 6). After the first 10 minutes glaze with honey glaze*.

*See 'Glazes' on page 26

CARROT TEA BREAD**

This is an unusual loaf and the ingredients can be varied. A brown flour makes a more substantial loaf. As there is a high proportion of oil in the recipe, make sure when baking that you test it with a skewer, otherwise the bread may be too damp. It is better *not* to wrap this loaf in foil before putting it in a tin. Keep a day. Cut thick and butter for tea.

2 Small Loaves

Ingredients

8 oz (M 225 gm, A 2 C) plain white cake flour

4 oz (M 115 gm, A 1 C) soft brown sugar

2 tsp (M 2 tsp, A 2½ tsp) ground cinnamon

2 tsp (M 2 tsp, A 2½ tsp) bicarbonate of soda

½ tsp (M ½ tsp, A ¾ tsp) salt

3 oz (M 85 gm, A 1/3 C) currants or chopped stoneless raisins or walnuts

6 oz (M 170 gm, A 1½ C) carrots grated as fine as possible

2 beaten eggs with:

2 tsp (M 2 tsp, A 2½ tsp) vanilla essence

½ pint (M ¼ litre, A 1¼ C) corn oil

Method

1. Put all the ingredients in a bowl and mix together by hand or machine until blended.

2. Pour into two small loaf tins, lined with foil.

3. Bake at 300°F (160°C, Gas Mark 2) for 1 hour until firm and dry when tested with a skewer.

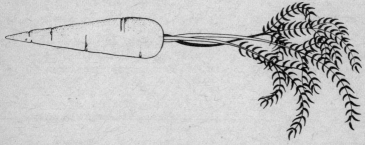

Yorkshire Tea Cakes**

I have a childhood memory of these delicious cakes. They were large and flat and we ate them warm and fresh, cut in slices like bread, spread thickly with farm butter. They should be toasted if over one day old, and they can also be used to make a splendid bread and butter pudding.

4 Large Tea Cakes

Ingredients

2 lb (M 1 kg, A 8 C) strong white bread flour

2 tsp (M 2 tsp, A 2½ tsp) salt

2 oz (M 55 gm, A 3 cake) fresh yeast

2 oz (M 55 gm, A ¼ C) lard

3·table (M 3 table, A 3¾ table) caster sugar

1 pint (M ½ litre, A 2½ C) luke-warm milk and water mixed

12 oz (M 350 gm, A 2 C) mixed dried fruit

Method

1. Put the flour and salt in a large bowl.
2. Rub in the lard and add the fruit and 2 table (M 2 table, A 2½ table) caster sugar.
3. Cream the yeast with the remaining sugar and a little milk.
4. Leave to froth for 5 minutes.
5. Pour yeast mixture into well.
6. Mix, adding sufficient liquid to make a kneadable dough.
7. Knead well.
8. Rise inside a closed polythene bag until doubled in size.
9. Knock back and shape into 4 round cakes.
10. Place on greased and floured tins.
11. Prove inside a closed polythene bag for 20 minutes.
12. Glaze with milk and bake at 425°F (220°C, Gas Mark 7) for 20 minutes.
13. Brush with sugar syrup when taken out of the oven.

HOT CROSS BUNS***

The international Good Friday bun. Hot Cross Buns tend to lose their crosses in the process of proving and baking. Mark firmly when the shaped buns are set to prove.

16 Buns

Ingredients

1 lb (M 450 gm, A 4 C) plain strong white flour

1 oz (M 30 gm, A 1½ cake) fresh yeast

½ pint (M ¼ litre, A 1½ C) warm milk

1 tsp (M 1 tsp, A 1¼ tsp) salt

1 rounded tsp (M 1 tsp, A 1¼ tsp) mixed spice

½ tsp (M ½ tsp, A ¾ tsp) grated nutmeg

2 oz (M 55 gm, A ¼ C) caster sugar

4 oz (M 115 gm, A 2/3 C) currants

2 oz (M 55 gm, A 1/3 C) peel, chopped fine

2 oz (M 55 gm, A ¼ C) melted margarine

Sugar to glaze*

*See 'Toppings' on page 26

Method

1. Put flour, salt, spices and sugar into a bowl.
2. Cream the yeast with a little milk and leave until frothy.
3. Add to the flour.
4. Pour the rest of the ingredients into the flour.
5. Mix well and knead to a smooth dough.
6. Rise for 2 hours in a closed polythene bag.
7. Turn the dough out onto a floured board and roll into a long sausage. Cut off pieces each the size of a ping-pong ball.
8. Roll into rounds under the hands.
9. Mark with a cross by using the back of a knife, and place on greased tins. Mark fairly deeply otherwise the impressions will 'rise' out.
10. Prove inside a closed polythene bag for 30 minutes.
11. Brush with milk.
12. Bake at 425°F (220°C, Gas Mark 7) for 15-20 minutes. Turn the tins around in the oven to brown evenly.
13. On removal from the oven, glaze with milk and sugar glaze.

The Storing of Bread

Home made bread does not have the long life of commercial bread, and care should be taken to ensure that containers are free from mould spores. Sterilize the containers with boiling water to ensure keeping your bread mould free. Tins can be sterilized in a very hot oven. Plastic containers should be rinsed out with boiling water every few weeks. Bread keeps moist if it is sealed in a plastic bag and stored in the fridge.

Batches of rolls and loaves freeze well sealed in plastic bags for 6 months. Rolls can be popped under a low grill in their frozen state, or in a low oven until soft. They do not retain their softness, however, and become harder and drier with successive reheatings.

Failures and How to Prevent Them

It helps to know why your finished loaf may not turn out as you thought it would.

Here are a few faults, their causes and prevention.

1. *A 'flying top' to the loaf:*
   The crust has pulled up on one side, giving the loaf an uneven top. The bread has not been allowed to rise fully in the tin. Allow longer for proving, and do not let the dough become too warm while proving.

2. *Dry and close textured loaf:*
   The rising time was insufficient for the dough. It should be allowed to double its bulk.

3. *Crumbly and open textured loaf:*
   Over-proved in the tin—cut the time down and don't prove in too warm a place. It also helps to increase the fat in the recipe: 1 oz fat (M 30 gm, A 2 table) per 2½ lb flour (M 1¼ kg, A 10 C).

4. *Heavy and dull looking white bread:*
   Insufficient kneading. The importance of thorough kneading cannot be over-emphasised. All types of bread will turn out looking like a 'door stop' if this part of bread-making is skimped.

5. *A hole in the centre of the loaf:*
   Air has been trapped in a fold of the dough—careful kneading and shaping is essential. Holes can also be caused by over-proving in the tin.

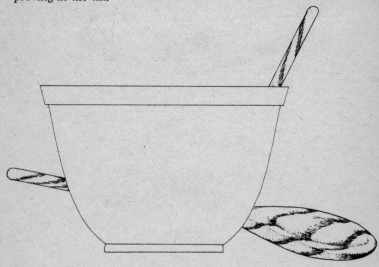

Index